THE FOLKTALE CAT

THE FOLKTALE CAT

Edited by **Frank de Caro**

Illustrations by **Kitty Harvill**

BARNES & NOBLE BOOKS
NEW YORK

This edition published by Barnes & Noble, Inc.,
by arrangement with August House.

1995 Barnes & Noble Books

ISBN 1-56619-776-7

Printed and bound in the United States of America

M 9 8 7 6 5 4 3 2

For

Bee, Pye, Robin, Lucy, Tom, Bobcat, Susan,
Nick, Dolly, Willie, Bob, Carl,
Yo-Yo, Elliott, Taffe, Katze, Jim,
Matty and Whitey

Acknowledgments

The editor and publisher would like to thank the owners of copyright material for permission to reprint the following stories:

"Why the Cat Falls on Her Feet," reprinted by permission of Wm. B. Eerdmans Publishing Co., from *Legends of Green Hill Sky*, by Louise Jean Walker, ©1959 by Wm. B. Eerdmans Publishing Co.

"The Cat and the 'Jam'," translated from the original Spanish by permission of the American Folklore Society, Inc., from *Folk-lore from the Dominican Republic*, by Manual J. Andrade (Memoirs of the American Folklore Society, vol. 23).

"The Cat, the Dog, and Death," from *The Piece of Fire and Other Haitian Tales*, Copyright 1942, 1964 by Harold Courlander.

"The Baldheaded Cat of Kowashi," reprinted from *Japanese Legends and Folk-Tales* by Yoshimatsu Suzuki, with the kind permission of Masayoshi Suzuki.

"Who Let the Cat Out of the Bag in Austin, Texas," by Diane Rutt, reprinted by permission of Diane Rutt from *The Texan Woman*, 1, no. 3 (April-May 1974).

"King Cat," and "The Lazy Cat," reprinted by permission of Artisjus Agency for Literature and Theatre, from *Hungarian Folk Tales*, edited by Gyula Ortutay, ©1962 by Corvina, Budapest.

"The Linguistic Cat," reprinted from *Pass the Port: The Best After-Dinner Stories of the Famous*, ©1976 Christian Brann, Ltd. Reprinted by permission of Dr. Valerie MacKay.

The editor would also like to thank Lorre Weidlich, Jan Brunvand, Joe Goodwin, Jay Edwards, Anna Nardo, Margaret Parker, Juan Barroso VIII, Morris Witten, the Vances (Ruth, Steve, Brigid, Netty, Ansel, and Kitty Kurti), and especially Robin Roberts for assistance.

Contents

THE
FOLKTALE
CAT

On Folktale Cats and Folklore

If asked with what in the world of folklore they associate cats, many people might reply that they think of witches, or of Halloween, or of the bad luck associated with black cats crossing paths.

Indeed, there is a long tradition connecting the cat and the witch. Certainly from the late Middle Ages, cats were popularly assumed to be witches' familiars (demons in animal or human form who served a witch, receiving their sustenance by sucking her blood), although in some accounts, the Devil appears to a witch in the form of a cat. The Halloween tie-in probably stems from the witchcraft connection. As a holiday, Halloween grew out of the ancient Celtic festival called Samhain. This was the day of the New Year but also the occasion when, it was thought, the souls of those who had died during the year made their way to the otherworld. Hence the night was filled with spirits and ghosts and other strange folk, like witches and their cat familiars.

The belief linking a black cat crossing one's path with bad luck is a widely known superstition today, and many also know that the bad luck can be counteracted by changing directions and going back. In the larger realm of folk tradition, however, cats, black and otherwise, have had other, often more beneficent meanings: on the coast of Yorkshire, fishermen's wives kept cats as luck charms to keep their husbands safe at sea; English football teams would sometimes carry a black cat onto the field for luck; noticing when a cat washes behind its ears was thought to be a handy way of predicting rain; and in various parts of England a visit from a black cat brings good luck, not bad.

Yet there is another important folkloric role cats fill, and that is as characters in folktales. In fairy tales and legends and anecdotes cats make their appearances to help worthy heroes, interact with other animals, or, indeed, assume a more terrifying mien as agents of the supernatural world. In Stith Thompson's *Motif Index of Folk Literature*—which refers us to the beings and the events of the world's folk narratives—cats fill nearly two pages of entries (and wild relatives like lions and tigers fill several more).

This popularity may have several reasons behind it, but first a word on folktales in general seems called for. In its broadest meaning the term *folktale* refers to a variety of those orally told stories which pass from person to person and from group to group by "word of mouth" and which for millenia have served as one means of satisfying the human hunger for narrative. *Fairy tales*—those fantasies of quests and magical transformations, of superhuman tasks and spectacular rewards—were the short story and the novel for the "pre-literate" peoples of Indo-Europe. These tales enchanted (and, even today, in some places, enchant) solely through the spoken work, a skilled narrator perhaps holding forth for hours or even nights on end in darkened villages whose inhabitants sought entertainment in a time before television or radio, in a world which books little penetrated. On the other hand, *legends*—stories of supposedly true, if bizarre or amazing, events, like the sighting of ghosts or the appearance of monsters—brought a kind of news into people's lives, but a news that could be especially savored in the telling and the wondering at. Humorous *jests* and *anecdotes* could and can evoke the laughter that comes only from the spinning of plots of elaborate mistakes or of foolish characters or through lampooned dialect.

Through virtually incessant retelling, oral stories were reshaped to fit new circumstances and creative urges and spread across the face of the earth (though the reshapings meant that the "same" tale might be told rather differently in different corners of the globe). Though today most Americans know some of these tales, like the fairy stories, only from the printed page, they were the staples of people's lives, providing entertainment and knowledge, exercising the imagination, and bringing, if indirectly, understanding and enlightenment. Today, though literacy is widespread and entertainment is available through mass media, we continue to tell stories, for word of mouth still seems the most appropriate medium for some kinds of narration. The spoken word seems best for "encoding" some of our hopes and anxieties, as in the strange "urban legends," those stories that recount events that supposedly happened to "a friend of a friend" and that circulate on campuses, in offices, and in other familiar modern contexts and tell of bizarre realities—of frightening killers, microwaved creatures, and alligators found in sewers.

But why have cats come to play a prominent role on the stage of oral narrative? One may suggest several possible attractions.

As the social historian Robert Darnton has noted, "there is an indefinable *je ne sais quoi* about cats, a mysterious something that has fascinated mankind since the time of the ancient Egyptians." Cats seem to us to be amalgams of alternate, even opposing qualities, cute yet cunning, domestic yet hunters, tame yet ferocious. They are, of course, animals, yet there is something peculiarly human about them. We suspect, as Darnton has put it, "a quasi-human intelligence behind a cat's eyes," and their "piercing and eerie" cry can seem strangely human too. Their cry and their "oddly independent" nature, folklorist Venetia Newall has suggested, may be partly why they have been associated with witchcraft, and all these factors may have something to do with their appearance in folktales.

Take, for example, their independence and the fact that they live with us humans, yet seem part of some other world too. Could that idea be better expressed than by the tale called "The King o' the Cats," a story told in various European countries as well as in the United States? Usually in this story, a cat is resting peacefully by the fire, the very picture of domesticity in a peaceful household. Suddenly someone brings news to the house that he has just seen a strange sight, a cortege of cats carrying a coffin to a grave while declaring that Tom Tildrum—or some such name—was dead. The heretofore calmly dozing house cat leaps up and announces that if that is true, he is now King of the Cats, and he disappears from the household to be seen no more. He has been leading, it would seem, parallel lives, one in our familiar human world, where he is merely a gentle fixture by the hearth, another in some unknown cat world, where he is a monarch and where cats live like humans, with funeral ceremonies and a line of royal succession. It is as we always suspected, that there is some mysterious other reality beyond the cat's "everyday" life and of which we get in the tale only a fleeting, unearthly glimpse.

The same is intimated in "The White Cat." This story as printed here is taken from Madame d'Aulnoy's French collection of the seventeenth century, but it is known from many cultures. The animal in the title role is not always a cat, yet the choice of a cat seems especially apt. Again, as the young prince enters the castle he has stumbled upon, we get the sense of a parallel cat world which has its many mysteries (though here there is a "logical" explanation for its existence—the white cat and her minions are an enchanted princess and her court). The cats of "The Colony of Cats" merely live in a deserted house, yet they seem to have their own society there, only peripherally connected to that of humankind.

But as often as not, cat characters are very much a part of our own human world, where they may prove invaluable assets to their owners (though many cat people will swear that no one ever truly owns a cat). Puss in Boots himself, the inheritance of an unpromising youngest son, takes charge of his human's life and makes his master's fortune. Bruno

Bettelheim, in *The Uses of Enchantment*, his famous psychological study of fairy tales and their great value to children, says that tales such as this one give a child confidence as he or she grows up. Puss's trickery in favor of his master does not, says Bettelheim, build character by promoting the choice of good over bad (as some other tales may) but rather provides "the hope that even the meekest can succeed in life," like the youngest son, with whom the small child, often feeling powerless indeed, can readily identify. The child learns that "little everyday events"—like "befriending an animal or being befriended by it"—may "lead to great things." And cats, of course—along with dogs—are the most familiar and domestic animals to a child. But the child will probably have discovered also that cats are independent, while the child himself is slowly trying to find the independence that gradually comes as we mature. A cat—such an independent creature—who helps a human find his own independence, as does Puss in Boots aid his master, may thus have a particular resonance for the child hearing the story. Then, too, he or she may find special comfort in a story in which help comes from an animal the child may think of as a bit aloof, as cats may sometimes appear to be. If aid can come even from a source as shy as a cat, then the world is indeed a place full of assisting forces, even unexpected ones, and there can be much security and comfort in that realization. Perhaps adult cat lovers will not find it surprising that Puss in Boots takes charge of his master's life, for don't their own felines often seem to do the same, if in less obvious ways?

Another invaluable cat is the one Dick Whittington takes to a cat-less land overrun by mice. Sir Richard Whittington was a real Lord Mayor of London (he died in 1423), but the story is a widely circulated folktale which, in its English incarnation, became attached to this historic personage. Why this should have happened is an interesting question—the great mythologist Max Müller thought it the result of linguistic confusion whereby the French word *achat*, meaning *trade*, in which Whittington had really made his fortune, was mistaken by the English for *a cat*—but it is not uncommon for certain real people to become characters in folktales. More interesting is the possible significance of the tale itself.

Social historian Darnton has ventured the opinion that fairy tales rather accurately, if indirectly, reflect the world of the European peasants who told such stories several centuries ago. On the one hand the world of their villages was a static and immobile one, where little changed from year to year, where their opportunities for advancement were severely limited and where they labored constantly. On the other hand, if they took to the road, as many were forced to do for want of land or work or even food at home, they faced many dangers from wild animals, criminals, and the natural elements in a land that was still a kind of frontier, with vast forest tracts and often no effective rule of law.

The tales are full of impoverished characters who venture out into life, and the stories often show that "the world is harsh and dangerous." Yet they also suggest how to survive and even prosper in such a world. One does so through using one's wits. (Puss in Boots is perhaps the consummate example.) But one also must venture forth from the static realm of the peasant village, despite the dangers inherent in such a move, to where the opportunities are more promising. Thus so many folktale heroes with unpromising prospects go forth to find success (and do).

Dick Whittington is one such unpromising protagonist who winds up making his fortune. That he does so through his cat seems especially appropriate. Cats, of course, were useful animals, but their usefulness was perhaps less obvious and direct than that of other domestic beasts. They did not provide food directly for the table, as would cows and chickens, nor such a readily observable service as dogs provided by standing guard over the household or herding cattle or sheep. They provided the very valuable service of fending off the rats and mice who compete with humans for the food supply and who might, in the case of rats, threaten in other ways. Perhaps this important task is alluded to in some versions of the British ballad "The Elfin Knight," where a cat carries grain to a mill, but the cat's general helpfulness was a rather silent, even secret service, and one not so readily remembered. The Whittington story reminds the hearer of that crucial service, but in doing so also makes clear how an unpromising hero—like the cat—may have powers that are not so readily apparent at first glance. Perhaps the same idea is suggested in that strange redaction of "Cinderella" known as "Catskin," wherein the heroine is known by that name because she wears the skin of a cat. She is the female equivalent of the adventuring but unpromising hero, though she seeks her fortune in a different way. Her catskin raiment is an odd touch which may in part reflect the magical powers attributed to cats, but it is also suggestive of her hidden will to triumph, unrealized, like the cat's great utility to humanity, at first glance.

Folktale cats come in various shapes and guises. Sometimes they take on positively human characteristics, sometimes they are depicted as the animals they are (though the touch of humanity that seems a part of them may lie very close to the surface). They may stand for cunning and wit, as in "Puss in Boots," or for the triumph of lives that seem unpromising as in Dick Whittington story. They may be harbingers of the world of the supernatural, as in "The Witch Cat" or "The Vampire Cat" of Nabéshima. They may symbolize the natural order, as in "Mouse and Mouser," wherein the cat acts as he does because it is her very nature to do so, suggesting that we cannot change what, fundamentally, as a species we are (an idea not unrelated to the well known proverb about a jungle cat, "A leopard can't change its spots"). They play roles in humorous stories, like the tale of the cat who became the most handsomest young man in the world, and in frightening stories like Ireland's "The Demon Cat." They may be protective, as in the Raja Rasâlu tale and "The Story of the Faithful Cat"; mysterious as in "The King o' the Cats"; or even cheaters, as in "The Cat and the Mouse in Partnership." Cats lovers may find these many roles appropriate, for cats seem to have many personalities, to show us many different sides. Indeed, cats may be the folktale animals par excellence: shape shifters who can translate themselves into countless forms.

The folk stories found in this book are varied in nature. Though the folktale is defined as an orally told story, these stories have often been written down. Since the Middle Ages writers like Chaucer and Boccaccio created literature out of this narrative folklore, and in the seventeenth century Charles Perrault and others began to create collections of folk stories they retold in print. Some of the stories in *The Folktale Cat* are literary retellings. At the beginning of the nineteenth century, however, the Grimm Brothers began to stimulate ever-growing interest in the actual *study* of oral tales. Though Jakob and Wilhelm Grimm edited and changed in various ways the stories they recorded from oral tradition to publish in their famous collection, the *Kinder- und Hausmärchen* (1812), the scholarly interest they themselves took, and which they encouraged in others, led tale collectors more and more to try to record the tales as they were told, seeing them as cultural documents best understood on their own terms. (In recent years, sound recording equipment and even video cameras have made this approach more effective as recording has been done in those parts of the world where oral tale-telling still survives and often flourishes.)

Some of the stories in this collection were written down by collectors who attempted to accurately reproduce the tales as told. However the tales were recorded for us, we hope that they will provide enjoyment for the reader. They have been reproduced here almost unchanged from the sources in which they originally appeared to preserve the efforts and the motives of those who originally collected or reworked them; only very minor editorial changes have been made for the sake of clarity and consistency. The nation or cultural area from which each tale comes is also indicated; this refers, however, only to the particular *version* of the story printed here, as nearly all of the stories are, in different versions, found in many other places as well.

Further information on folktales and on the stories in this collection can be found in the Afterword.

According to a Chinese legend cats once ruled the world, but one day a council of the wisest cats decided it wasn't worth the effort. So they turned the job over to the next highest form of animal life—man. And cats have been retired ever since.
—Newspaper filler item

The cat among Mahomedans is cherished since the day when a snake got into Mahomed's sleeve, and the Prophet said, "Get out!" and he refused. For then the Prophet said, "Let us refer the matter to the cat," and the snake consented. And the cat said to the snake, "Put out your head and let us talk the matter over." And when the snake put out his head, the cat pounced on him, and carried him off. Therefore, say the people, a cat should never be struck except with a cotton-ball!
—Charles Swynnerton, *Indian Nights' Entertainment*

On the Nature of Cats (and Some Other Creatures)

THE POPULAR IMAGINATION has assigned certain domestic and wild beasts fixed symbolic meanings or has established notions of their fundamental animal natures. Perhaps no beast has figured more in this process than the cat, and what we suppose to be facets of the feline are central to a number of folktales.

Thus the *hunter* cat (who may be asked even by leopards for instruction in how to catch chase prey!) cannot resist pouncing on a mouse, even if the mouse is supposedly its partner; and another cat—turned into a maiden in one of Aesop's fables—must put aside human lovemaking to pursue a rodent that happens upon the scene. The *cunning* cat may feign holiness to capture a meal, pretend to be a godmother in order to steal food, or intrigue to devour her neighbors. The *mysterious* cat lives both in the world known to humans and in a shadowy "otherworld" in which there are cat kings and royal funerals. The *smug* cat may take the place of the overconfident hare and lose a race (not to a tortoise, but to a crab).

The tales of this section tell us of various cat characteristics and relationships, of why dogs and cats are enemies, why cats live inside and dogs outside houses, why cats are smaller than their lion cousins (because they have had to live with those most domineering creatures of all—human beings), and why cats land on their feet when they fall. In the course of things our cats may display not only their own natures (or, rather, our human conceptions of their natures) but also show up those of other, fellow creatures: dogs, mice, men, lions, leopards (indeed, the two African stories in this section of the book give different accounts of why those wild cats, leopards, appear to be one-sided hunters).

Those who feel they know cats well can decide for themselves how apt these symbolic portraits may be.

The Cat and the Mouse in Partnership

[ENGLAND]

A cat had made acquaintance with a mouse and had spoken so much of the great love and friendship she felt for her, that at last the mouse consented to live in the same house with her and to go shares in the housekeeping.

"But we must provide for the winter or else we shall suffer hunger," said the cat. "You, little Mouse, cannot venture everywhere in case you run at last into a trap."

This good counsel was followed, and a little pot of fat was bought. But they did not know where to put it.

At length, after long consultation, the cat said, "I know of no place where it could be better put than in the church. No one will trouble to take it away from there. We will hide it in a corner, and we won't touch it till we are in want."

So the little pot was placed in safety; but it was not long before the cat had a great longing for it, and said to the mouse, "I wanted to tell you, little Mouse, that my cousin has a little son, with white and brown spots, and she wants me to be godmother to it. Let me go out today, and do you take care of the house alone."

"Yes, go certainly," replied the mouse, "and when you eat anything good, think of me: I should very much like a drop of the red christening wine."

But it was all untrue. The cat had no cousin, and had not been asked to be godmother. She went straight to the church, slunk to the little pot of fat, began to lick it, and licked the top off. Then she took a walk on the roofs of the town, looked at the view, stretched herself out in the sun, and licked her lips whenever she thought of the little pot of fat. As soon as it was evening she went home again.

"Ah, here you are again!" said the mouse. "You must certainly have had an enjoyable day."

"It went off very well," answered the cat.

"What was the child's name?" asked the mouse.

"Top Off," said the cat dryly.

"Topoff!" echoed the mouse. "It is indeed a wonderful and curious name. Is it in your family?"

"What is there odd about it?" said the cat. "It is not worse than Breadthief, as your godchild is called."

Not long after this another great longing came over the cat. She said to the mouse, "You must again be kind enough to look after the house alone, for I have been asked a second time to stand godmother, and as this child has a white ring round its neck, I cannot refuse."

The kind mouse agreed, but the cat slunk under the town wall to the church, and ate up half of the pot of fat. "Nothing tastes better," said she, "than what one eats by oneself," and she was very much pleased with her day's work.

When she came home the mouse asked, "What was this child called?"

"Half gone," answered the cat.

"Halfgone! What a name! I have never heard it in my life. I don't believe it is in the calendar of saints' days."

Soon the cat's mouth began to water once more after her licking business. "All good things in threes," she said to the mouse. "I have again to stand godmother. The child is quite black, and has very white paws, but not a single white hair on its body. This only happens once in two years, so you will let me go out?"

"Topoff! Halfgone!" repeated the mouse. "They are such curious names; they make me very thoughtful."

"Oh, you sit at home in your dark grey coat and your long tail," said the cat, "and you get fanciful. That comes of not going out in the day."

The mouse had a good cleaning out while the cat was gone, and made the house tidy; but the greedy cat ate the fat every bit up.

"When it is all gone, one can be at rest," she said to herself, and at night she came home sleek and satisfied. The mouse asked at once after the third child's name.

"It won't please you any better," said the cat, "he was called Clean Gone."

"Cleangone!" repeated the mouse. "I do not believe that name has been printed any more than the others. Cleangone! What can it mean?"

She shook her head, curled herself up, and went to sleep.

From this time on no one asked the cat to stand godmother; but when the winter came and there was nothing to be got outside, the mouse remembered their provision and said, "Come, Cat, we will go to our pot of fat which we have stored away; it will taste very good."

"Yes, indeed," answered the cat. "It will taste as good to you as if you stretched your thin tongue out of the window."

They started off, and when they reached it they found the pot in its place, but quite empty!

"Ah," said the mouse, "now I know what has happened! It has all come out! You are a true friend to me! You have eaten it all when you stood godmother; first the top off, then half of it gone, then...."

"Will you be quiet!" screamed the cat. "Another word and I will eat you up."

"Cleangone" was already on the poor mouse's tongue, and scarcely was it out than the cat made a spring at her, seized and swallowed her.

You see, that is the way of the world.

Four of Aesop's Fables

In ancient Greece, collections of fables were attributed to Aesop, probably a semi-legendary figure; these stories, thought to have teaching value, came to have morals attached to them.

A Cat and Venus

A young fellow that was passionately in love with a cat made it his humble suit to Venus to turn puss into a woman. The transformation was wrought in the twinkling of an eye, and out she comes, a very bucksome lass. The doting sot took her home to his bed and bad fair for a litter of kittens by her that night. But as the loving couple lay snugging together, a fancy took Venus in the head, to try to see if the cat had changed her manners with her shape and so, for experiment, turned a mouse loose into the chamber. The cat, upon this temptation, started out of the bed and, without any regard to the marriage joys, made a leap at the mouse, which Venus took for so high an affront that she turned the madam into a puss again.

MORAL: *The extavagant transports of love and the wonderful force of nature are unaccountable; the one carries us out of ourselves, and the other brings us back again.*

The Eagle, the Cat, and the Sow

An eagle had built her nest upon the top branches of an old oak. A wild cat inhabited a hole in the middle; and in the hollow part at the bottom was a sow, with a whole litter of pigs. A happy neighborhood and might long have continued so, had it not been for the wicked insinuations of the designing cat. For, first of all, up she crept to the eagle.

"Good neighbor," says she, "we shall all be undone. That filthy sow yonder does nothing but lie routing at the foot of the tree, and, as I suspect, intends to grub it up, that she may the more easily come at your young ones. For my part I will take care of my own concerns; you may do as you please, but I will watch her motions, though I stay at home this month for it."

When she had said this, which could not fail of putting the eagle into a great fright, down she went, and made a visit to the sow at the bottom, putting on a sorrowful face.

"I hope," says she, "you do not intend to go abroad today?"

"Why not?" says the sow.

"Nay," replies the other, "you may do as you please; but I overheard the eagle tell her young ones that she would treat them with a pig the first time she saw you go out, and I am not sure but she may take up with a kitten in the meantime; so, goodmorrow to you; you will excuse me, I must go and take care of the little folks at home."

Away she went accordingly; and, by contriving to steal out softly at nights for her prey, and to stand watching and peeping all day at her hole, as under great concern, she made such an impression on the eagle and the sow, that neither of them dared to venture abroad for fear of the other, the consequence of which was that themselves and their young ones, in a little time, were all starved, and made prize of by the treacherous cat and her kittens.

MORAL: *There can be no peace in any state or family where whisperers and talebearers are encouraged.*

The Cat and the Fox

As the cat and the fox were talking politics together, on a time, in the middle of the forest, Reynard the Fox said, let things turn out ever so bad, he did not care, for he had a thousand tricks for them yet before they should hurt him.

"But pray," says he, "Mrs. Puss, suppose there should be an invasion, what course do you design to take?"

"Nay," says the cat, "I have but one shift for it; and if that won't do, I am undone."

"I am sorry for you," replies Reynard, "with all my heart, and would gladly furnish you with one or two of mine, but indeed, neighbor, as times go, it is not good to trust; we must even be everyone for himself, as the saying is."

These words were scarce out of his mouth, when they were alarmed with a pack of hounds that came upon them full cry. The cat, by the help of her single shift, ran up a tree, and sat securely among the top branches, from whence she beheld Reynard, who had not been able to get out of sight, overtaken by his thousand tricks, and torn in as many pieces by the dogs which had surrounded him.

MORAL: *Successful cunning often makes an ostentatious pretension to wisdom.*

Belling the Cat

Long ago, the mice held a general council to consider what measures they could take to outwit their common enemy, the cat. Some said this, and some said that; but at last a young mouse got up and said he had a proposal to make, which he thought would meet the case.

"You will agree," said he, "that our chief danger consists in the sly and treacherous manner in which the enemy approaches us. Now, if we could receive some signal of her approach, we could easily escape from her. I venture, therefore, to propose that a small bell be procured, and attached by a ribbon round the neck of the cat. By this means we should always know when she was about, and could easily retire while she was in the neighborhood."

This proposal met with general applause, until an old mouse got up and said: "That is all very well, but who is to bell the cat?"

The mice looked at one another and nobody spoke. Then the old mouse said:

MORAL: *"It is easy to propose impossible remedies."*

The King o' the Cats
[ENGLAND]

One winter's evening the sexton's wife was sitting by the fireside with her big black cat, Old Tom, on the other side, both half asleep and waiting for the master to come home. They waited and they waited, but still he didn't come, till at last he came rushing in, calling out, "Who's Tommy Tildrum?" in such a wild way that both his wife and his cat stared at him to know what was the matter.

"Why, what's the matter?" said his wife. "And why do you want to know who Tommy Tildrum is?"

"Oh, I've had such an adventure. I was digging away at old Mr. Fordyce's grave when I suppose I must have dropped asleep, and only woke up by hearing a cat's *miaou*."

"Miaou!" said Old Tom in answer.

"Yes, just like that! So I looked over the edge of the grave, and what do you think I saw?"

"Now, how can I tell?" said the sexton's wife.

"Why, nine black cats all like our friend Tom here, all with a white spot on their chestesses. And what do you think they were carrying? Why, a small coffin covered with a black velvet pall, and on the pall was a small coronet all of gold, and at every third step they took they cried all together, 'Miaou...' "

"Miaou!" said Old Tom again.

"Yes, just like that!" said the Sexton. "And as they came nearer and nearer to me I could see them more distinctly, because their eyes shone out with a sort of green light. Well, they all came towards me, eight of them carrying the coffin, and the biggest cat of all walking in front for all the world like—but look at our Tom, how he's looking at me. You'd think he knew all I was saying."

"Go on, go on," said his wife; "never mind Old Tom."

"Well, as I was a-saying, they came towards me slowly and solemnly, and at every third step crying all together, 'Miaou...' "

"Miaou!" said Old Tom again.

"Yes, just like that, till they came and stood right opposite Mr. Fordyce's grave, where I was, when they all stood still and looked straight at me. I did feel queer, that I did! But look at Old Tom; he's looking at me just like they did."

"Go on, go on," said his wife; "never mind Old Tom."

"Where was I? Oh, they all stood looking at me, when the one that wasn't carrying the coffin came forward and, staring straight at me, said to me—yes, I tell 'ee, said to me, with a squeaky voice, 'Tell Tom Tildrum that Tim Toldrum's dead,' and that's why I asked you if you knew who Tom Tildrum was, for how can I tell Tom Tildrum Tim Toldrum's dead if I don't know who Tom Tildrum is?"

"Look at Old Tom, look at Old Tom!" screamed his wife.

And well he might look, for Tom was swelling and Tom was staring, and at last Tom shrieked out, "What—old Tim dead! then I'm the King o' the Cats!" and rushed up the chimney and was never more seen.

Why the Cat Falls on Her Feet
[NATIVE AMERICAN]

Manabozho is a culture hero of North Central Woodland groups, including the Chippewa; he figures in many tales, and in the third paragraph there is an allusion to events in another story.

I'm too tired to walk farther in this forest until I get some rest," said Manabozho wearily.

The sun was high overhead when Manabozho lay down on the ground at the foot of a tree. Soft, green moss grew all about him. The sun shone through the leaves and made spots of light and shadow on the ground. As he lay resting, he heard the songs of the birds, the buzz and the hum of insects, and the wind rustling the leaves of the trees. A feeling of peace and quietness stole over Manabozho, and soon all the music of the forest lulled him to sleep.

While Manabozho slept, a large, poisonous snake came gliding noiselessly through the grass. It lifted its head and saw Manabozho lying at the foot of the tree. "I will kill him," it hissed. "I could have eaten that cat yesterday, if that man hadn't called out, 'Watch, little cat, watch!' Now it will be his turn to feel my fangs!"

Closer and closer crept the poisonous snake. Manabozho stirred in his sleep. He mumbled, "Watch, little cat, watch!" At this warning, the snake withdrew, but soon noticing that Manabozho's eyes were shut fast, it again went closer, and made ready to strike.

Manabozho did not move.

Upon a high branch of a tree directly above Manabozho's head lay a little cat. She had seen the snake when it came from the thicket, and had watched it glide through the grass and draw closer and closer to Manabozho. She heard it hiss.

The little cat's body quivered with anger and shook with fear, for she was very tiny indeed. "Manabozho has been very good to me," she thought. "I cannot let the great snake bite him." And in the next instant, she had leapt down upon the ugly monster.

Oh, how angry the snake was! It hissed and its eyes were like balls of fire as it lashed out wildly at the little cat. The brave cat leapt again and again upon the snake's head until, at last, the snake lay dead beside the sleeping Manabozho.

When Manabozho awoke, the cat was lying near the dead snake, and Manabozho realized at once that this cat had saved his life.

He stroked her gently and said, "You brave creature! You saved my life. What can I do to show my gratitude, and to honor you for your brave fight?"

At last he exclaimed, "I know what I shall do! You have sharp eyes and keen ears. You can run swiftly. Hereafter, you shall be known over all the earth as the friend of Man, and you shall always have a home in Man's home. You jumped from the high tree to kill the poisonous snake. Now as long as you live, you shall be able to leap wherever you will and always fall upon your feet."

Why the Leopard Can Only Catch Prey on Its Left Side
[GHANA]

At one time leopards did not know how to catch animals for food. Knowing that the cat was very skillful in this way, Leopard one day went to Cat and asked very politely if she would teach him the art. Cat readily consented.

The first thing Leopard had to learn was to hide himself among the bushes by the roadside, so that he would not be seen by any animal passing by. Next, he must learn how to move noiselessly through the woods. He must never allow the animal he chased to know that he was following it. The third great principle was how to use his left paws and side in springing upon his prey.

Having taught him these three things, Cat requested him to go and practice them well. When he had learnt them throroughly he could return to her and she would give him more lessons in hunting.

Leopard obeyed. At first he was very successful and obtained all the food he wanted. One day, however, he was unable to catch anything at all.

Being very hungry, he bethought himself what he could have for dinner. Suddenly he remembered that the cat had quite a large family. He went straight to her home and found her absent.

Never thinking of her kindness to him—Leopard only remembered that he was hungry—he ate all her kittens. Puss, on discovering this dreadful fact, was so angry that she refused to have anything more to do with the great creature.

Consequently the leopard has never been able to learn how to catch animals that pass him on the right side.

The Cat and the "Jam"
[DOMINICAN REPUBLIC]

There was a cat that was always playing with the dog. The cat taught him how to steal and taught him to run but never taught him how to climb. One day the dog was mistreating the cat, and the cat got mad.

When the cat got really fed up, he climbed up to a treetop, and the dog said to the cat, "Why didn't you teach me to climb?"

And the cat said, "The last trick the cat doesn't teach to the dog."

The dog left and the cat came down. And one day in the morning the cat heard someone saying, "Oh, my God! What a jam!"

And the cat got curious. He didn't know what "a jam" was. He never had gone hungry, always grabbing what didn't belong to him. At last one day the cat resolved to find out what "a jam" was. He started to think and think by the seashore. And he got on a boat and went to where God is.

When he arrived where God is, the cat said to him, "Mr. God, I came here before you, so you could tell me what 'a jam' is."

God said to him: "Sit down."

And after about three days of sitting there, God gave him a sack and a suitcase and told him, "Take this. Until you get to a big grassy plain, don't open the suitcase. But be sure to look around and see that there is not even one tree around."

And the cat left very happy. He walks and walks, looking for the grassy plain.

He came across a poor old man and he said, "Do you know where there is a large grassy plain where there is not even one tree?"

The old man said, "Certainly, there is one near here. Over there on the other side of that hill that you see over there—right there."

And the cat arrives over there and he enters the grassy plain and walks and walks until he doesn't see a tree. Already the cat was very hungry. And he looked all around and didn't even find a small bush.

He was so happy with the suitcase that God gave him so he could know what "a jam" was. So happy he was that he forgot that he was carrying food. He put down the suitcase and wanted to open it with both hands, but then he thought, "No, I am going to open it with just one hand." He was very happy about his surprise!

When he opened the suitcase in the place where there was not even one tree, a bulldog jumped out. What a sight! The cat felt trapped, looking to all sides to see if he could find at least a bush to climb. And the dog behind him ready to attack him. At last God goes and places a little tree for him to climb. And in that way he was able to escape.

And the cat said, "If this is 'a jam,' I don't want to know any more about it."

The Cat, the Dog, and Death
[HAITI]

*I*n ancient times, in the beginning of things, God had not yet made up his mind about whether the creatures he had created should live forever. The question had not yet been decided.

The cat and the dog had a discussion about the matter.

The cat said, "It is my opinion that when creatures have lived their lives, they should not go on living forever."

The dog said, "Oh, no, on the contrary—I think that we should live for all time."

"No," the cat insisted, "No one should live forever. When he has lived his life, that is enough."

The dog said, "I will go to see God about this matter. I shall insist that all creatures should live forever."

The cat declared, "I too will go to see God about this question."

They parted. The dog considered how he could delay the cat. He took some butter, placed it on a banana leaf, and set it by the edge of the trail where the cat would not miss seeing it.

As for the cat, he too considered how he might delay the dog. He found a large bone and placed it near the trail where the dog would not fail to see it. He went home, bathed himself, and dressed. Then he began the journey to God's house.

The dog also bathed and dressed and set out for God's house.

When the cat came to the place where the butter was waiting for him, he ignored it and continued on his way.

When the dog came to the place where the bone was waiting for him, he smelled it. He said to himself, "This is no time to stop." But as he passed the bone, his head turned so that his nose was pointing directly at it. He stopped and sat down. He said to his nose, "This is no time for pointing." He started out again, but his head turned further and further, until his nose was pointing backwards toward his tail. At last the dog went back and began to gnaw on the bone.

The cat arrived at God's house. God asked him, "What is it you have come to tell me?"

The cat replied, "I have come to say that when a person has lived out his life, then he should live no longer."

God thought about the matter. At last he said, "Very well, so it shall be."

When the dog had finished gnawing on the bone, he continued on his way to God's house. God asked him, "What is it you have come to tell me?"

The dog answered, "I have come to say that all creatures should live forever."

But God said, "It is too late. The decision has been made."

So it is that no creature lives forever. Because the dog could not resist the bone lying by the trail, he did not arrive in time. With the dog it is still this way. He cannot pass a bone anywhere without giving it a great deal of attention.

Cat Adventurers and Adventures with Cats

WHEN THEY THINK OF "FOLKTALES," perhaps most people will have in mind those stories of fantastic adventures, of princes, dragons and ogres, and of journeys into exotic lands where castles magically disappear or houses are made of gingerbread. Indeed, such stories—in English most commonly called fairy tales—might be said to stand at the center of folktale-telling, jewels polished by countless fascinated recountings over the course of many, many years.

Cats make their various appearances in such tales of adventure. They may take on human characteristics while yet keeping their feline attributes too—Puss in Boots, one of the many helpful animals of the fairy tale world, dons footwear and intrigues for his master while he also remembers how to hunt small game and retires to a leisurely life of chasing mice for pleasure. They may be transformed humans, as is the princess in "The White Cat," or be transformed into humans, as in the Indian story of the cat who becomes a queen through the intervention of a goddess. Or they may simply stay quite in their animal forms and yet help human adventurers by their very cat natures—by ridding a hitherto cat-less land of rat invaders or by guarding a hero from attack by a powerful rat.

The stories which follow in this section have in common some sort of adventure, whether to a land on the far side of the globe, to a mysterious castle, or just to "a deserted house not far from ... town." One tale, the celebrated English "Catskin," does not, strictly speaking, contain a cat character at all, and some readers may be horrified that the main character wears a robe made of cat fur. Yet the inherent symbolism of the Cinderella-like heroine's being disguised like a cat seemed to suggest an underlying awareness of hidden power—like those we sometimes suspect cats possess—and may say something too about the identification of cats with women and the feminine. Thus this story too seemed an appropriate inclusion.

The Master Cat; or, Puss in Boots
[FRANCE]

There was a miller who left no more estate to the three sons he had than his mill, his ass, and his cat. The partition was soon made. Neither the scrivener nor attorney was sent for. They would soon have eaten up all the poor patrimony. The eldest had the mill, the second the ass, and the youngest nothing but the cat.

The poor young fellow was quite comfortless at having so poor a lot.

"My brothers," said he, "may get their living handsomely enough by joining their stocks together; but, for my part, when I have eaten up my cat, and made me a muff of his skin, I must die of hunger."

The cat, who heard all this, but made as if he did not, said to him with a grave and serious air:

"Do not thus afflict yourself, my good master; you have nothing else to do but to give me a bag, and get a pair of boots made for me, that I may scamper through the dirt and the brambles, and you shall see that you have not so bad a portion of me as you imagine."

The cat's master did not build very much upon what he said; he had, however, often seen him play a great many cunning tricks to catch rats and mice, as when he used to hang by the heels, or hide himself in the meal, and make as if he were dead; so that he did not altogether despair of his affording him some help in his miserable condition. When the cat had what he asked for, he booted himself very gallantly, and, putting his bag about his neck, he held the two strings of it in his two forepaws, and went into a warren where was a great abundance of rabbits. He put bran and sow-thistle into his bag, and, stretching out at length, as if he had been dead, he waited for some young rabbits, not yet acquainted with the deceits of the world, to come and rummage his bag for what he had put into it.

Scarce was he lain down but he had what he wanted: a rash and foolish young rabbit jumped into his bag, and Monsieur Puss, immediately drawing closed the strings, took and killed him without pity. Proud of his prey, he went with it to the palace, and asked to speak with His Majesty. He was shown upstairs into the king's apartment, and, making a low reverance, said to him:

"I have brought you, sir, a rabbit of the warren, of which my noble Lord, the Master of Carabas" (for that was the title which Puss was pleased to give his master) "has commanded me to present to Your Majesty from him."

"Tell thy master," said the king, "that I thank him, and that he does me a great deal of pleasure."

Another time he went and hid himself among some standing corn, holding still his bag open; and, when a brace of partridges ran into it, he drew the strings, and so caught them both. He went and made a present of these to the king, as he had done before of the rabbit which he took in the warren. The king, in like manner, received the partridges with great pleasure, and ordered him some money, to drink.

The cat continued for two or three months thus to carry His Majesty, from time to time, game of his master's taking. One day in particular, when he knew for certain that the king was to take the air along the river-side, with his daughter, the most beautiful princess in the world, he said to his master:

"If you will follow my advice your fortune is made. You have nothing else to do but go and wash yourself in the river, in that part I shall show you, and leave the rest to me."

The Marquis of Carabas did what the cat advised him to, without knowing why or wherefore. While he was washing, the king passed by, and the cat began to cry out:

"Help! help! My Lord Marquis of Carabas is going to be drowned."

At this noise the king put his head out of the coach-window, and, finding it was the cat who had so often brought him such good game, he commanded his guards to run immediately to the assistance of his Lordship the Marquis of Carabas. While they were drawing the poor marquis out of the river, the cat came up to the coach and told the king that, while his master was washing, there came by some rogues, who went off with his clothes, though he had cried out: "Thieves! Thieves!" several times, as loud as he could.

This cunning cat had hidden them under a great stone. The king immediately commanded the officers of his wardrobe to run and fetch one of his best suits for the Lord Marquis of Carabas.

The king caressed him after a very extraordinary manner, and, as the fine clothes he had given him extremely set off his good mien (for he was well made and very handsome in his person), the king's daughter took a secret inclination to him, and the Marquis of Carabas had no sooner cast two or three respectful and somewhat tender glances but she fell in love with him to distraction. The king would needs have him come into the coach and take part of the airing. The cat, quite overjoyed to see his project begin to succeed, marched on before, and, meeting with some countrymen, who were mowing a meadow, he said to them:

"Good people, you who are mowing, if you do not tell the king that the meadow you mow belongs to my Lord Marquis of Carabas, you shall be chopped as small as herbs for the pot."

The king did not fail asking of the mowers to whom the meadow they were mowing belonged.

"To my Lord Marquis of Carabas," answered they altogether, for the cat's threats had made them terribly afraid.

"You see, sir," said the marquis, "this is a meadow which never fails to yield a plentiful harvest every year."

The Master Cat, who went still on before, met with some reapers, and said to them:

"Good people, you who are reaping, if you do not tell the king that all this corn belongs to the Marquis of Carabas, you shall be chopped as small as herbs for the pot."

The king, who passed by a moment after, would needs know to whom all that corn, which he then saw, did belong.

"To my Lord Marquis of Carabas," replied the reapers, and the king was very well pleased with it, as well as the marquis, whom he congratulated thereupon. The Master Cat, who went always before, said the same words to all he met, and the king was astonished at the vast estates of my Lord Marquis of Carabas.

Monsieur Puss came at last to a stately castle, the master of which was an ogre, the richest had ever been known; for all the lands which the king had then gone over belonged to this castle. The cat, who had taken care to inform himself who this ogre was and what he could do, asked to speak with him, saying he could not pass so near his castle without having the honor of paying his respects to him.

The ogre received him as civilly as an ogre could do, and made him sit down.

"I have been assured," said the cat, "that you have the gift of being able to change yourself into all sorts of creatures you have a mind to; you can, for example, transform yourself into a lion, or elephant, or the like."

"That is true," answered the ogre very briskly, "and to convince you, you shall see me now become a lion."

Puss was so sadly terrified at the sight of a lion so near him that he immediately got into the gutter of the roof, not without an abundance of trouble and danger, because of his boots, which were of no use at all to him in walking upon the tiles. A little while after, when Puss saw the ogre had resumed his natural form, he came down, and owned he had been very much frightened.

"I have been moreover informed," said the cat, "but I know not how to believe it, that you have also the power to take on you the shape of the smallest animals; for example, to change yourself into a rat or a mouse; but I must own to you that I take this to be impossible."

"Impossible!" cried the ogre. "You shall see that presently."

And at the same time he changed himself into a mouse, and began to run about the floor. Puss no sooner perceived this but he fell upon him and ate him up.

Meanwhile the king, who saw, as he passed, this fine castle of the ogre's, had a mind to go into it. Puss, who heard the noise of His Majesty's coach running over the drawbridge, ran out, and said to the king:

"Your Majesty is welcome to this castle of my Lord Marquis of Carabas."

"What! my Lord Marquis," cried the king, "and does this castle also belong to you? There can be nothing finer than this court and all the stately buildings which surround it; let us go into it, if you please."

The marquis gave his hand to the princess and followed the king, who went first. They passed into a spacious hall, where they found a magnificent collation, which the ogre had prepared for his friends, who were that very day to visit him, but dared not to enter, knowing the king was there. His Majesty was perfectly charmed with the good qualities of my Lord Marquis of Carabas, as was his daughter, who had fallen violently in love with him, and, seeing the vast estate he possessed, said to him, after having drunk five or six glasses:

"It will be owing to yourself only, my Lord Marquis, if you are not my son-in-law."

The marquis, making several low bows, accepted the honor which His Majesty conferred upon him, and forthwith, that very same day, married the princess.

Puss became a great lord, and never ran after mice anymore but only for his diversion.

The White Cat
[*FRANCE*]

Once upon a time there was a king who had three sons, who were all so clever and brave that he began to be afraid that they would want to reign over the kingdom before he was dead. Now the king, though he felt that he was growing old, did not at all wish to give up the government of his kingdom while he could still manage it very well, so he thought the best way to live in peace would be to divert the minds of his sons by promises which he could always get out of when the time came for keeping them.

So he sent for them all, and, after speaking to them kindly, he added:

"You will quite agree with me, my dear children, that my great age makes it impossible for me to look after my affairs of state as carefully as I once did. I begin to fear that this may affect the welfare of my subjects, therefore I wish that one of you should succeed to my crown; but in return for such a gift as this it is only right that you should do something for me. Now, as I think of retiring into the country, it seems to me that a pretty, lively, faithful little dog would be very good company for me; so, without any regard for your ages, I promise that the one who brings me the most beautiful little dog shall succeed me at once.

The three princes were greatly surprised by their father's sudden fancy for a little dog, but as it gave the two younger ones a chance they would not otherwise have had of being king, and as the eldest was too polite to make any objection, they accepted the commission with plea-sure. They bade farewell to the king, who gave them presents of silver and precious stones, and appointed to meet them at the same hour, in the same place, after a year had passed, to see the little dogs they had brought for him.

Then they went together to a castle which was about a league from the city, accompanied by all their particular friends, to whom they gave a grand banquet, and the three brothers promised to be friends always, to share whatever good fortune befell them, and not to be parted by any envy or jealousy; and so they set out, agreeing to meet at the same castle at the appointed time, to present themselves before the king together. Each one took a different road, and the two eldest met with many adventures; but it is about the youngest that you are going to hear. He was young, and gay, and handsome, and knew everything that a prince ought to know; and as for his courage, there was simply no end to it.

Hardly a day passed without his buying several dogs—big and little, greyhounds, mastiffs, spaniels, and lapdogs. As soon as he had bought a pretty one he was sure to see a still prettier, and then he had to get rid of all the others and buy that one, as, being alone, he found it impossible to take thirty or forty dogs about with him. He journeyed from day to day, not knowing where he was going, until at last, just at nightfall, he reached a great, gloomy forest. He did not know his way, and, to make matters worse, it began to thunder, and the rain poured down. He took the first path he could find, and after walking for a long time he fancied he saw a faint light and began to hope that he was coming to some cottage where he might find shelter for the night. At length, guided by the light, he reached the door of the most splendid castle he could have imagined. The door was of gold covered with carbuncles, and it was the pure red light which shone from them that had shown him the way through the forest. The walls were of the finest porcelain in all the most delicate colors, and the prince saw that all the stories he had ever read were pictured upon them; but as he was quite terribly wet, and the rain still fell in torrents, he could not stay to look about anymore, but came back to the golden door. There he saw a deer's foot hanging by a chain of diamonds, and he began to wonder who could live in this magnificant castle.

"They must feel very secure about robbers," he said to himself. "What is to hinder anyone from cutting off that chain and digging out those carbuncles, and making himself rich for life?"

He pulled the deer's foot and immediately a silver bell sounded and the door flew open, but the prince could see nothing but numbers of hands in the air, each holding a torch. He was so much surprised that he stood quite still, until he felt himself pushed forward by other hands, so that, though he was somewhat uneasy, he could not help going on. With his hand on his sword, to be prepared for whatever might happen, he entered a hall paved with lapis lazuli, while two lovely voices sang:

> The hands you see floating above
>   Will swiftly your bidding obey;
> If your heart dreads not conquering Love,
>   In this place you may fearlessly stay.

The prince could not believe that any danger threatened him when he was welcomed in this way, so, guided by the mysterious hands, he went towards a door of coral, which opened of its own accord, and he found himself in a vast hall of mother-of-pearl, out of which opened a number of other rooms, glittering with thousands of lights, and full of such beautiful pictures and precious things that the prince felt quite bewildered. After passing through sixty rooms the hands that conducted him stopped, and the prince saw a most comfortable-looking armchair drawn up close to the chimney corner; at the same moment the fire lighted itself, and the pretty, soft, clever hands took off the prince's wet, muddy clothes, and presented him with fresh ones made of the richest stuffs, all embroidered with gold and emeralds. He could not help admiring everything he saw, and the deft way in which the hands waited on him, though they sometimes appeared so suddenly that they made him jump.

When he was quite ready—and I can assure you that he looked very different from the wet and weary prince who had stood outside in the rain and pulled the deer's foot—the hands led him to a splendid room, upon the walls of which were painted the histories of Puss in Boots and a number of other famous cats. The table was laid for supper with two golden plates, and golden spoons and forks, and all the sideboard was covered with dishes and glasses of crystal set with precious stones. The prince was wondering who the second place could be for, when suddenly in came about a dozen cats carrying guitars and rolls of music. They took their places at one end of the room and, under the direction of a cat who beat time with a roll of paper, began to mew in every imaginable key, and to draw their claws across the strings of the guitars, making the strangest kind of music that could be heard. The prince hastily stopped up his ears, but even then the sight of these comical musicians sent him into fits of laughter.

"What funny thing shall I see next?" he said to himself, and instantly the door opened, and in came a tiny figure covered by a long black veil, and he saw that it was the loveliest little white cat it is possible to imagine. She looked very young and very sad, and in a sweet little voice that went straight to his heart she said to the prince:

"King's son, you are welcome; the Queen of the Cats is glad to see you."

"Lady Cat," replied the prince, "I thank you for receiving me so kindly, but surely you are no ordinary pussycat? Indeed, the way you speak and the magnificence of your castle prove it plainly."

"King's son," said the White Cat, "I beg you to spare me these compliments, for I am not used to them. But now," she added, "let supper be served, and let the musicians be silent, as the prince does not understand what they are saying."

So the mysterious hands began to bring in the supper, and first they put on the table two dishes, one containing stewed pigeons and the other a fricassee of fat mice. The sight of the latter made the prince feel as if he could not enjoy his supper at all; but the White Cat, seeing this, assured him that the dishes intended for him were prepared in a separate kitchen, and he might be quite certain that they contained neither rats nor mice; and the prince felt so sure that she would not deceive him that he had no more hesitation in the beginning. Presently he noticed that on the little paw that was next him the White Cat wore a bracelet containing a portrait, and he begged to be allowed to look at it. To his great surprise he found it represented an extremely handsome young man, who was so like himself that it might have been his own portrait! The White Cat sighed as he looked at it, and seemed sadder then ever, and the prince dared not ask any questions for fear of displeasing her; so he began to talk about other things, and found that she was interested in all the subjects he cared for himself, and seemed to know quite well what was going on in the world. After supper they went into another room, which was fitted up as a theatre, and the cats acted and danced for their amusement, and then the White Cat said goodnight to him, and the hands conducted him into a room he had not seen before, hung with tapestry worked with butterflies' wings of every color; there were mirrors that reached from the ceiling to the floor, and a little white bed with curtains of gauze tied up with ribbons.

The prince went to bed in silence, as he did not quite know how to begin a conversation with the hands that waited on him, and in the morning he was awakened by a noise and confusion outside his window, and the hands came and quickly dressed him in hunting costume. When he looked out, all the cats were assembled in the courtyard, some leading greyhounds, some blowing horns, for the White Cat was going out hunting. The hands led a wooden horse up to the prince, and seemed to expect him to mount it, at which he was very indignant; but it was no use for him to object, for he speedily found himself upon its back, and it pranced gaily off with him.

The White Cat was riding a monkey, which climbed even up to the eagles' nests when she had a fancy for the young eaglets. Never was there a pleasanter hunting party, and when they returned to the castle the prince and the White Cat supped together as before, but when they had finished she offered him a crystal goblet, which must have contained a magic draught, for, as soon as he had swallowed its contents, he forgot everything, even the little dog that he was seeking for the king, and only thought how happy he was with the White Cat! And so the days passed, in every kind of amusement, until the year was nearly gone. The prince had forgotten all about meeting his brothers; he did not even know what country he belonged to; but the White Cat knew when he ought to go back, and one day she said to him:

"Do you know that you have only three days left to look for the little dog for your father, and your brothers have found lovely ones?"

Then the prince suddenly recovered his memory, and cried:

"What can have made me forget such an important thing? My whole fortune depends upon it; and even if I could in such a short time find a dog pretty enough to gain me a kingdom, where should I find a horse who could carry me all that way in three days?" And he began to be very vexed.

But the White Cat said to him: "King's son, do not trouble yourself; I am your friend, and will make everything easy for you. You can still stay here for a day, as the good wooden horse can take you to your country in twelve hours."

"I thank you, beautiful Cat," said the prince, "but what good will it do me to get back if I have not a dog to take to my father?"

"See here," answered the White Cat, holding up an acorn, "there is a prettier one in this than in the Dog-star."

"Oh! White Cat dear," said the prince, "how unkind you are to laugh at me now!"

"Only listen," she said, holding to acorn to his ear.

And inside he distinctly heard a tiny voice say: "Bow wow!"

The prince was delighted, for a dog that can be shut up in an acorn must be very small indeed. He wanted to take it out and look at it, but the White Cat said it would be better not to open the acorn till he was before the king, in case the tiny dog should be cold on the journey. He thanked her a thousand times, and said goodbye quite sadly when the time came for him to set out.

"The days have passed so quickly with you," he said, "I only wish I could take you with me now."

But the White Cat shook her head and sighed deeply in answer.

After all, the prince was the first to arrive at the castle where he had agreed to meet his brothers, but they came soon after, and stared in amazement when they saw the wooden horse in the courtyard jumping like a hunter.

The prince met them joyfully, and they began to tell him all their adventures; but he managed to hide from them what he had been doing, and even led them to think that a turnspit dog which he had with him was the one he was bringing for the king. Fond as they all were of one another, the two eldest could not help being glad to think that their dogs certainly had a better chance. The next morning they started in the same chariot. The elder brothers carried in baskets two such tiny, fragile dogs that they hardly dared to touch them. As for the turnspit, he ran after the chariot, and got so covered with mud that one could hardly see what he was like at all.

When they reached the palace everyone crowded round to welcome them as they went into the king's great hall; and when the two brothers presented their little dogs nobody could decide which was the prettier. They were already arranging between themselves to share the kingdom equally, when the youngest stepped forward, drawing from his pocket the acorn the White Cat had given him. He opened it quickly, and there, upon a white cushion, they saw a dog so small that it could easily have been put through a ring. The prince laid it upon the ground, and it got up at once and began to dance. The king did not know what to say, for it was impossible that anything could be prettier than this little creature. Nevertheless, as he was in no hurry to part with his crown, he told his sons that, as they had been so successful the first time, he would ask them to go once again, and seek by land and sea for a piece of muslin so fine that it could be drawn through the eye of a needle. The brothers were not very willing to set out again, but the two eldest consented because it gave them another chance, and they started as before. The youngest again mounted the wooden horse, and rode back at full speed to his beloved White Cat. Every door of the castle stood wide open, and every window and turret was illuminated, so it looked more wonderful than before. The hands hastened to meet him, and led the wooden horse off to the stable, while he hurried to find the White Cat. She was asleep in a little basket on a white satin cushion, but she very soon started up when she heard the prince, and was overjoyed at seeing him once more.

"How could I hope that you would come back to me, king's son?" she said. And then he stroked and petted her, and told her of his successful journey, and how he had come back to ask her help, as he believed that it was impossible to find what the king demanded. The White Cat looked serious, and said she must think what was to be done, but that, luckily, there were some cats in the castle who could spin very well, and if anybody could manage it they could, and she would set them upon the task herself.

And then the hands appeared carrying torches, and conducted the prince and the White Cat to a long gallery which overlooked the river, from the windows of which they saw a magnificent display of fireworks of all sorts; after which they had supper, which the prince liked even better that the fireworks, for it was very late, and he was hungry after his long ride. And so the days passed quickly as before; it was impossible to feel dull with the White Cat, and she had quite a talent for inventing new amusements—indeed, she was more clever than any cat has a right to be. But when the prince asked her how it was that she was so wise, she only said:

"King's son, do not ask me; guess what you please. I may not tell you anything."

The prince was so happy that he did not trouble himself at all about the time, but presently the White Cat told him that the year was gone, and that he need not be at all anxious about the piece of muslin, as they had made it very well.

"This time," she added, "I can give you a suitable escort." And on looking out into the courtyard the prince saw a superb chariot of burnished gold, enamelled in flame color with a thousand different devices. It was drawn by twelve snow-white horses, harnessed four abreast; their trappings were of flame-colored velvet, embroidered with diamonds. A hundred chariots followed, each drawn by eight horses, and filled with officers in splendid uniforms, and a thousand guards surrounded the procession.

"Go!" said the White Cat. "And when you appear before the king in such state he surely will not refuse you the crown which you deserve. Take this walnut, but do not open it until you are before him, then you will find in it the piece of stuff you asked me for."

"Lovely Blanchette," said the prince, "how can I thank you properly for all your kindness to me? Only tell me that you wish it, and I will give up forever all thought of being king, and will stay here with you always."

"King's son," she replied, "it shows the goodness of your heart that you should care so much for a little white cat, who is good for nothing but to eat mice; but you must not stay."

So the prince kissed her little paw and set out. You can imagine how fast he travelled when I tell you that they reached the king's palace in just half the time it had taken the wooden horse to get there. This time the prince was so late that he did not try to meet his brothers at their castle, so they thought he could not be coming, and were rather glad of it, and displayed their pieces of muslin to the king proudly, feeling sure of success. And indeed the stuff was very fine, and would go through the eye of a very large needle; but the king, who was only too glad to make a difficulty, sent for a particular needle, which was kept among the crown jewels, and had such a small eye that everybody saw at once that it was impossible that the muslin should pass through it. The princes were angry, and were beginning to complain that it was a trick, when suddenly the trumpets sounded and the youngest prince came in. His father and brothers were quite astonished at his magnificence, and after he had greeted them he took the walnut from his pocket and opened it, fully expecting to find the piece of muslin, but instead there was only a hazelnut. He cracked it, and there lay a cherrystone. Everybody was looking on, and the king was chuckling to himself at the idea of finding the piece of muslin in a nutshell.

However, the prince cracked the cherrystone, but everyone laughed when he saw it contained only its own kernel. He opened that and found a grain of wheat, and in that was a millet seed. Then he himself began to wonder and muttered softly:

"White Cat, White Cat, are you making fun of me?"

In an instant he felt a cat's claw give his hand quite a sharp scratch, and hoping that it was meant as an encouragement he opened the millet seed, and drew out of it a piece of muslin four hundred ells long, woven with the loveliest colours and most wonderful patterns; and when the needle was brought it went through the eye six times with the greatest ease! The king turned pale, and the other princes stood silent and sorrowful, for nobody could deny that this was the most marvellous piece of muslin that was to be found in the world.

Presently the king turned to his sons and said, with a deep sigh:

"Nothing could console me more in my old age than to realize your willingness to gratify my wishes. Go then once more, and whoever at the end of a year can bring back the loveliest princess shall be married to her, and shall, without further delay, receive the crown, for my successor must certainly be married."

The prince considered that he had earned the kingdom fairly twice over, but still he was too well bred to argue about it, so he just went back to his gorgeous chariot, and, surrounded by his escort, returned to the White Cat faster than he had come. This time she was expecting him; the path was strewn with flowers, and a thousand braziers were burning scented woods which perfumed the air. Seated in a gallery from which she could see his arrival, the White Cat waited for him.

"Well, king's son," she said, "here you are once more, without a crown."

"Madam," said he, "thanks to your generosity I have earned one twice over; but the fact is that my father is so loath to part with it that it would be no pleasure to me to take it."

"Never mind," she answered, "it's just as well to try and deserve it. And as you must take back a lovely princess with you next time, I will be on the lookout for one for you. In the meantime let us enjoy ourselves; tonight I have ordered a battle between my cats and the river rats, on purpose to amuse you." So this year slipped away even more pleasantly than the preceding ones. Sometimes the prince could not help asking the White Cat how it was she could talk.

"Perhaps you are a fairy," he said. "Or has some enchanter changed you into a cat?"

But she only gave him answers that told him nothing. Days go by so quickly when one is very happy that it is certain the prince would never have thought of its being time to go back, when one evening as they sat together the White Cat said to him that if he wanted to take a lovely princess home with him the next day he must be prepared to do as she told him.

"Take this sword," she said, "and cut off my head!"

"I!" cried the prince. "I cut off your head! Blanchette darling, how could I do it?"

"I entreat you to do as I tell you, king's son," she replied.

The tears came into the prince's eyes as he begged her to ask him anything but that—to set him any task she pleased as a proof of his devotion, but to spare him the grief of killing his dear Pussy. But nothing he could say altered her determination, and at last he drew his sword, and desperately, with a trembling hand, cut off the little white head. But imagine his astonishment and delight when suddenly a lovely princess stood before him, and, while he was still speechless with amazement, the door opened and a goodly company of knights and ladies entered, each carrying a cat's skin! They hastened with every sign of joy to the princess, kissing her hand and congratulating her on being once more restored to her natural shape. She received them graciously, but after a few minutes begged that they would leave her alone with the prince, to whom she said:

"You see, Prince, that you were right in supposing me to be no ordinary cat. My father reigned over six kingdoms. The queen, my mother, whom he loved dearly, had a passion for travelling and exploring, and when I was only a few weeks old she obtained his permission to visit a certain mountain of which she had heard many marvelous tales, and set out, taking with her a number of her attendants. On the way they had to pass near an old castle belonging to the fairies. Nobody had ever been into it, but it was reported to be full of the most wonderful things, and my mother remembered to have heard that the fairies had in their garden such fruits as were to be seen nowhere else. She began to wish to try them for herself, and turned her steps in the direction of the garden. On arriving at the door, which blazed with gold and jewels, she ordered her servants to knock loudly, but it was useless; it seemed as if all the inhabitants of the castle must be asleep or dead. Now the more difficult it became to obtain the fruit, the more the queen was determined that have it she would. So she ordered that they should bring ladders, and get over the wall into the garden; but though the wall did not look very high, and they tied the ladders together to make them very long, it was quite impossible to get to the top.

"The queen was in despair, but as night was coming on she ordered that they should encamp just where they were, and went to bed herself, feeling quite ill, she was so disappointed. In the middle of the night she was suddenly awakened, and saw to her surprise a tiny, ugly old woman seated by her bedside, who said to her:

" 'I must say that we consider it somewhat troublesome of Your Majesty to insist upon tasting our fruit; but, to save you any annoyance, my sisters and I will consent to give you as much as you can carry away, on one condition—that is, that you shall give us your little daughter to bring up as our own.'

" 'Ah! my dear madam,' cried the queen, 'is there nothing else that you will take for the fruit? I will give you my kingdoms willingly.'

" 'No,' replied the old fairy, 'we will have nothing but your little daughter. She shall be as happy as the day is long, and we will give her everything that is worth having in fairy-land, but you must not see her again until she is married.'

" 'Though it is a hard condition,' said the queen, 'I consent, for I shall certainly die if I do not taste the fruit, and so I should lose my little daughter either way.'

"So the old fairy led her into the castle, and, though it was still the middle of the night, the queen could see plainly that it was far more beautiful than she had been told, which you can easily believe, Prince," said the White Cat, "when I tell you that it was this castle that we are now in. 'Will you gather the fruit yourself, Queen?' said the old fairy, 'or shall I call it to come to you?'

" 'I beg you to let me see it come when it is called,' cried the queen; 'that will be something quite new.' The old fairy whistled twice, then she cried:

" 'Apricots, peaches, nectarines, cherries, plums, pears, melons, grapes, apples, oranges, lemons, gooseberries, strawberries, raspberries, come!'

"And in an instant they came tumbling in, one after another, and yet they were neither dusty nor spoilt, and the queen found them quite as good as she had fancied them. You see they grew upon fairy trees.

"The old fairy gave her golden baskets in which to take the fruit away, and it was as much as four hundred mules could carry. Then she reminded the queen of her agreement, and led her back to the camp, and next morning she went back to her kingdom; but before she had gone very far she began to repent of her bargain, and when the king came out to meet her she looked so sad that he guessed that something had happened and asked him what was the matter. At first the queen was afraid to tell him, but when, as soon as they reached the palace, five frightful little dwarves were sent by the fairies to fetch me, she was obliged to confess what she had promised. The king was very angry, and had the queen and myself shut up in a great tower and safely guarded, and drove the little dwarves out of his kingdom; but the fairies sent a great dragon who ate up all the people he met, and whose breath burnt up everything as he passed through the country; and at last, after trying in vain to rid himself of the monster, the king, to save his subjects, was obliged to consent that I should be given up to the fairies. This time they came themselves to fetch me, in a chariot of pearl drawn by sea horses, followed by the dragon, who was led with chains of diamonds. My cradle was placed between the old fairies, who loaded me with caresses, and away we whirled through the air to a tower which they had built on purpose for me.

"There I grew up surrounded with everything that was beautiful and rare, and learning everything that is ever taught to a princess, but without any companions but a parrot and a little dog, who could both talk; and receiving every day a visit from one of the old fairies, who came mounted upon the dragon.

"One day, however, as I sat at my window, I saw a handsome young prince, who seemed to have been hunting in the forest which surrounded my prison, and who was standing and looking up at me. When he saw that I observed him he saluted me with great deference. You can imagine that I was delighted to have someone new to talk to, and in spite of the height of my window our conversation was prolonged till night fell, then my prince reluctantly bade me farewell. But after that he came again many times, and at last I consented to marry him, but the question was how I was to escape from my tower. The fairies also supplied me with flax for my spinning, and by great diligence I made enough cord for a ladder that would reach to the foot of the tower; but, alas! just as my prince was helping me to descend it, the crossest and ugliest of the old fairies flew in. Before he had time to defend himself my unhappy lover was swallowed up by the dragon. As for me, the fairies, furious at having their plans defeated, for they intended me to marry the king of the dwarves and I utterly refused, changed me into a white cat. When they brought me here I found all the lords and ladies of my father's court awaiting me under the same enchantment, while the people of lesser rank had been made invisible, all but their hands.

"As they laid me under the enchantment the fairies told me all my history, for until then I had quite believed that I was their child, and warned me that my only chance of regaining my natural form was to win the love of a prince who resembled in every way my unfortunate lover."

"And you have won it, lovely Princess," interrupted the prince.

"You are indeed wonderfully like him," resumed the princess, "in voice, in features, everything; and if you really love me all my troubles will be at an end."

"And mine too," cried the prince, throwing himself at her feet, "if you will consent to marry me."

"I love you already better than anyone in the world," she said; "but now it is time to go back to your father, and we shall hear what he says about it."

So the prince gave her his hand and led her out, and they mounted the chariot together; it was even more splendid than before, and so was the whole company. Even the horses' shoes were of rubies with diamond nails, and I suppose that is the first time such a thing was ever seen.

As the princess was as kind and clever as she was beautiful, you may imagine what a delightful journey the prince found it, for everything the princess said seemed to him quite charming.

When they came near the castle where the brothers were to meet, the princess got into a chair carried by four of the guards; it was hewn out of one splendid crystal and had silken curtains, which she drew round her that she might not be seen.

The prince saw his brothers walking upon the terrace, each with a lovely princess, and they came to meet him, asking if he also had found a wife. He answered that he had found something much rarer—a little white cat! At which they laughed very much, and asked him if he was afraid of being eaten up by mice in the palace. And they set out together for the town. Each prince and princess rode in a splendid carriage; the horses were decked with plumes of feathers and glittered with gold. After them came the youngest prince, and last of all the crystal chair, at which everybody looked with admiration and curiosity. When the courtiers saw them coming they hastened to tell the king.

"Are the ladies beautiful?" he asked anxiously.

And when they answered that nobody had ever before seen such lovely princesses he seemed quite annoyed.

However, he received them graciously, but found it impossible to choose between them.

Then turning to his youngest son he said:

"Have you come back alone, after all?"

"Your Majesty," replied the prince, "will find in that crystal chair a little white cat, which has such soft paws, and mews so prettily, that I am sure you will be charmed with it."

The king smiled, and went to draw back the curtains himself, but at a touch from the princess the crystal shivered into a thousand splinters, and there she stood in all her beauty; her fair hair floated over her shoulders and was crowned with flowers, and her softly falling robe was of the purest white. She saluted the king gracefully, while a murmur of admiration rose from all around.

"Sire," she said, "I am not come to deprive you of the throne you fill so worthily. I have already six kingdoms, permit me to bestow one upon you, and upon each of your sons. I ask nothing but your friendship, and your consent to my marriage with your youngest son; we shall have three kingdoms left for ourselves."

The king and all their courtiers could not conceal their joy and astonishment, and the marriage of the three princes was celebrated at once. The festivities lasted several months, and then each king and queen departed to their own kingdom and lived happily ever after.

The Cat Who Became a Queen
[*INDIA*]

Ah me! ah me! What availeth my marriage with all these women? Never a son has the Deity vouchsafed me. Must I die, and my name be altogether forgotten in the land?"

Thus soliloquised one of the greatest monarchs that ever reigned in Kashmir, and then went to his zanana [women's quarters], and threatened his numerous wives with banishment if they did not bear him a son within the next year. The women prayed most earnestly to the god Shiva to help them to fulfill the king's desire, and waited most anxiously for several months, hoping against hope, till at last they knew that it was all in vain, and that they must dissemble matters if they wished to remain in the royal household. Accordingly, on an appointed time, word was sent to the king that one of his wives was enceinte, and a little while afterwards the news was spread abroad that a little princess was born.

But this, as we have said, was not so. Nothing of the kind had happened. The truth was, that a cat had given birth to a lot of kittens, one of which had been appropriated by the king's wives. When His Majesty heard the news he was exceedingly glad, and ordered the child to be brought to him—a very natural request, which the king's wives had anticipated, and therefore were quite prepared with a reply.

"Go and tell the king," said they to the messenger, "that the Brahmans have declared that the child must not be seen by her father until she is married."

Thus the matter was hushed for a time.

Constantly did the king inquire after his daughter, and received wonderful accounts of her beauty and cleverness; so that his joy was great. Of course he would like to have had a son, but since the Deity had not condescended to fulfill his desire, he comforted himself with the thought of marrying his daughter to some person worthy of her, and capable of ruling the country after him. Accordingly, at the proper time he commissioned his counsellors to find a suitable match for his daughter. A clever, good, and handsome prince was soon found, and arrangements for the marriage were quickly concluded.

What were the king's wives to do now? It was of no use for them to attempt to carry on their deceit any longer. The bridegroom would come and would wish to see his wife, and the king, too, would expect to see her.

"Better," said they, "that we send for this prince and reveal everything to him, and take our chance of the rest. Never mind the king. Some answer can be made to satisfy him for a while."

So they sent for the prince and told him everything, having previously made him swear that he would keep the secret, and not reveal it even to his father or mother. The marriage was celebrated in grand style, as became such great and wealthy kings, and the king was easily prevailed on to allow the palanquin containing the bride to leave the palace without looking at her. The cat only was in the palanquin, which reached the prince's country in safety. The prince took great care of the animal, which he kept locked up in his own private room, and would not allow anyone, not even his mother, to enter it.

One day, however, while the prince was away, his mother thought that she would go and speak to her daughter-in-law from outside the door.

"Oh daughter-in-law," she cried, "I am very sorry that you are shut up in this room and not permitted to see anybody. It must be very dull for you. However, I am going out today; so you can leave the room without fear of seeing anyone. Will you come out?"

The cat understood everything, and wept much, just like a human being. Oh those bitter tears! They pierced the mother's heart, so that she determined to speak very strictly to her son on the matter as soon as he should return. They also reached the ears of the goddess Parvati, who at once went to her lord, Shiva, and entreated him to have mercy on the poor helpless cat.

"Tell her," said Shiva, "to rub some oil over her fur, and she will become a beautiful woman. She will find the oil in the room where she now is."

Parvati lost no time in disclosing this glad news to the cat, who quickly rubbed the oil over its body, and was changed into the most lovely woman that ever lived. But she left a little spot on one of her shoulders, which remained covered with cat's fur, lest her husband should suspect some treachery and deny her.

In the evening the prince returned and saw his beautiful wife, and was delighted. Then all anxiety as to what he should reply to his mother's earnest solicitations fled. She had only to see the happy, smiling, beautiful bride to know that her fears were altogether needless.

In a few weeks the prince, accompanied by his wife, visited his father-in-law, who, of course, believed the princess to be his own daughter, and was glad beyond measure. His wives too rejoiced, because their prayer had been heard and their lives saved. In due time the king settled his country on the prince, who eventually ruled over both countries, his father's and his father-in-law's, and then became the most illustrious and wealthy monarch in the world.

The Colony of Cats
[ITALY]

*L*ong, long ago, as far back as the time when animals spoke, there lived a community of cats in a deserted house not far from a large town. They had everything they could possibly desire for their comfort, they were well fed and well lodged, and if by any chance an unlucky mouse was stupid enough to venture in their way, they caught it, not to eat it but for the pure pleasure of catching it.

The old people of the town related how they had heard their parents speak of a time when the whole country was so overrun with rats and mice that not so much as a grain of corn nor an ear of maize was to be gathered in the fields; and it might be out of gratitude to the cats who had rid the country of these plagues that their descendants were allowed to live in peace.

No one knows where they got the money to pay for everything, nor who paid it, for all this happened so very long ago. But one thing is certain, they were rich enough to keep a servant, for though they lived very happily together, and did not scratch nor fight more than human beings would have done, they were not clever enough to do the housework themselves and preferred at all events to have someone to cook their meat, which they would have scorned to eat raw.

Not only were they very difficult to please about the housework, but most women quickly tired of living alone with only cats for companions, consequently they never kept a servant long; and it had become a saying

61

in the town, when anyone found herself reduced to her last penny: "I will go and live with the cats," and so many a poor woman actually did.

Now Lizina was not happy at home, for her mother, who was a widow, was much fonder of her older daughter. Often the younger one fared very badly and had not enough to eat, while the elder could have everything she desired, and if Lizina dared to complain she was certain to have a good beating.

At last the day came when she was at the end of her courage and patience and exclaimed to her mother and sister, "As you hate me so much you will be glad to get rid of me, so I am going to live with the cats!"

"Be off with you!" cried her mother, seizing an old broom-handle from behind the door.

Poor Lizina did not wait to be told twice, but ran off at once and never stopped till she reached the door of the cats' house. Their cook had left them that very morning, with her face all scratched, the result of such a quarrel with the head of the house that he had very nearly scratched out her eyes. Lizina therefore was warmly welcomed, and she set to work at once to prepare the dinner, not without many misgivings as to the taste of the cats, and whether she would be able to satisfy them.

Going to and fro about her work, she found herself frequently hindered by a constant succession of cats who appeared one after the other in the kitchen to inspect the new servant. She had one in front of her feet, another perched on the back of her chair while she peeled the vegetables, a third sat on the table beside her, and five or six others prowled about among the pots and pans on the shelves against the wall.

The air resounded with their purring, which meant they were pleased with their new maid, but Lizina had not yet learned to understand their language, and often she did not know what they wanted her to do. However, as she was a good, kind-hearted girl, she set to work to pick up the little kittens which tumbled about on the floor, she patched up quarrels, and nursed on her lap a big tabby—the oldest of the community—which had a lame paw.

All these kindnesses could hardly fail to make a favorable impression on the cats, and it was even better after a while, when Lizina had become accustomed to their strange ways. Never had the house been kept so clean, the meats so well served, nor the sick cats so well cared for.

After a time they had a visit from an old cat, whom they called their father, who lived by himself in a barn at the top of the hill, and came down from time to time to inspect the little colony. He too was much taken with Lizina and inquired, on first seeing her, "Are you well served by this nice, black-eyed little person?" and the cats answered with one voice, "Oh, yes, Father Gatto, we have never had so good a servant!"

At each of his visits the answer was always the same; but after a time the old cat, who was very observant, noticed that the little maid had grown to look sadder and sadder.

"What is the matter, my child—has anyone been unkind to you?" he asked one day, when he found her crying in her kitchen.

She burst into tears and answered between her sobs, "Oh, no! They are all very good to me. But I long for news from home and I pine to see my mother and my sister!"

Old Gatto, being a sensible old cat, understood the little servant's feelings.

"You shall go home," he said, "and you shall not come back unless you please. But first you must be rewarded for all your kind services to my children. Follow me down into the inner cellar, where you have never yet been, for I always keep it locked and carry the key away with me."

Lizina looked around her in astonishment as they went down into the great vaulted cellar underneath the kitchen. Before her stood the big earthenware water jars, one of which contained oil, the other a liquid shining like gold.

"Into which of these jars shall I dip you?" asked Father Gatto, with a grin that showed all his sharp white teeth, while his mustaches stood out straight on either side of his face.

The little maid looked at the two jars from under her long, dark lashes. "In the oil jar," she answered timidly, thinking to herself, "I could not ask to be bathed in gold."

But Father Gatto replied, "No, no; you have deserved something better than that."

And seizing her in his strong paws he plunged her into the liquid gold.

Wonder of wonders! When Lizina came out of the jar she shone from head to foot like the sun in the heavens on a fine summer's day. Her pretty pink cheeks and long black hair alone kept their natural color; otherwise she had become like a statue of pure gold.

Father Gatto purred loudly with satisfaction. "Go home," he said, "and see your mother and sister; but take care, if you hear the cock crow, to turn toward it; if on the contrary the ass brays, you must look the other way."

The little maid, having gratefully kissed the white paw of the old cat, set off for home; but just as she got near her mother's house the cock crowed, and quickly she turned toward it. Immediately a beautiful golden star appeared on her forehead, crowning her glossy black hair. At the same time the ass began to bray, but Lizina took care not to look over the fence into the field where the donkey was feeding. Her mother and sister, who were in front of their house, uttered cries of admiration and astonishment when they saw her, and their cries became still louder when Lizina, taking her handkerchief from her pocket, drew out also a handful of gold.

For some days the mother and her two daughters lived very happily together, for Lizina had given them everything she had brought away except her golden clothing, for that would not come off, in spite of all the efforts of her sister, who was madly jealous of her good fortune. The golden star, too, could not be removed from her forehead. But all the gold pieces she drew from her pockets had found their way to her mother and sister.

"I will go now and see what I can get out of the pussies," said Peppina, the elder girl, one morning, as she took Lizina's basket and fastened her pockets into her own skirt. "I should like some of the cats' gold for myself," she thought, as she left her mother's house before the sun rose.

The cat colony had not yet taken another servant, for they knew they could never get one to replace Lizina, whose loss they had not ceased to mourn. When they heard that Peppina was her sister, they all ran to meet her.

"She is not the least like her," the kittens whispered among themselves.

"Hush, be quiet!" the older cats said. "All servants cannot be pretty."

No, decidedly she was not at all like Lizina. Even the most reasonable and large-minded of the cats soon acknowledged that.

The very first day she shut the kitchen door in the face of the tomcats who used to enjoy watching Lizina at her work, and a young and mischievous cat who jumped in by the open kitchen window and alighted on the table got such a blow with the rolling pin that he squalled for an hour.

With every day that passed, the household became more and more aware of its misfortune.

The work was as badly done as the servant was surly and disagreeable. In the corners of the rooms there were collected heaps of dust;

spiders' webs hung from the ceilings and in front of the window panes; the beds were hardly ever made, and the feather beds, so beloved by the old and feeble cats, had never once been shaken since Lizina left the house. At Father Gatto's next visit he found the whole colony in a state of uproar.

"Caesar has one paw so badly swollen that it looks as if it were broken," said one. "Peppina kicked him with her great wooden shoes on. Hector has an abscess in his back where a wooden chair was flung at him; and Agrippina's three little kittens have died of hunger beside their mother, because Peppina forgot them in their basket up in the attic. There is no putting up with the creature—do send her away, Father Gatto! Lizina herself would not be angry with us; she must know very well what her sister is like."

"Come here," said Father Gatto, in his most severe tones, to Peppina. And he took her down into the cellar and showed her the same two great jars that he had showed Lizina. "Into which of these shall I dip you?" he asked.

And she made haste to answer: "In the liquid gold," for she was no more modest than she was good and kind.

Father Gatto's yellow eyes darted fire. "You have not deserved it," he uttered in a voice like thunder, and, seizing her, he flung her into the jar of oil, where she was nearly suffocated.

When she came to the surface screaming and struggling, the vengeful cat seized her again and rolled her in the ash-heap on the floor; then, when she rose, dirty, blinded and disgusting to behold, he thrust her from the door, saying, "Begone, and when you meet a braying ass be careful to turn your head toward it."

Stumbling and raging, Peppina set off for home, thinking herself fortunate to find a stick by the wayside with which to support herself. She was within sight of her mother's house when she heard in the meadow on the right the voice of a donkey loudly braying. Quickly she turned her head toward it and at the same time put her hand up to her forehead where, waving like a plume, was a donkey's tail. She ran home to her mother at the top of her speed, yelling with rage and despair; and it took Lizina two hours with a big basin of hot water and two cakes of soap to get rid of the layer of oil and ashes with which Father Gatto had adorned her. As for the donkey's tail, it was impossible to get rid of that; it was as firmly fixed on her forehead as was the golden star on Lizina's.

Their mother was furious. She first beat Lizina unmercifully with the broom, then she took her to the mouth of the well and lowered her into it, leaving her at the bottom, weeping and crying for help.

Before this happened, however, the king's son, in passing the mother's house, had seen Lizina sitting sewing in the parlor and had been dazzled by her beauty. After coming back two or three times, he at last ventured to approach the window and to whisper in the softest voice, "Lovely maiden, will you be my bride?"

And she had answered, "I will."

Next morning, when the prince arrived to claim his bride, he found her wrapped in a large white veil.

"It is so that maidens are received from their parents' hands," said the mother, who hoped to make the king's son marry Peppina in place of her sister and had fastened the donkey's tail round her head like a lock of hair under the veil.

The prince was young and a little timid, so he made no objections and seated Peppina in the carriage beside him.

Their way led past the old house inhabited by the cats, who were all at the window, for the report had got about that the prince was going to marry the most beautiful maiden in the world, on whose forehead shone a golden star, and they knew that this could only be their adored Lizina. As the carriage slowly passed in front of the old house, where cats from all parts of the world seemed to be gathered, a song burst from every throat:

> Mew, mew, mew!
> Prince, look quick behind you!
> In the well is fair Lizina,
> And you have nothing but Peppina.

When he heard this, the coachman, who understood the cat's language better than the prince, his master, stopped his horse and asked: "Does Your Highness know what the grimalkins are saying?"

The song broke forth again, louder than ever.

With a turn of his hand the prince threw back the veil and discovered the puffed-up, swollen face of Peppina, with the donkey's tail twisted round her head.

"Ah, traitress!" he exclaimed and, ordering his horses to turn around, he drove the elder daughter, quivering with rage, to the old woman who had sought to deceive him. With his hand on the hilt of his sword he demanded Lizina in so terrific a voice that the mother hastened to the well to draw the prisoner out.

Lizina's clothing and her star shone so brightly that when the prince led her home to the king, his father, the whole palace was lit up. Next day they were married and lived happily ever after; and all the cats, headed by Father Gatto, were present at the wedding.

Whittington and His Cat
[ENGLAND]

*I*n the reign of the famous King Edward III there was a little boy called Dick Whittington, whose father and mother died when he was very young, so that he remembered nothing at all about them and was left a ragged little fellow, running about a country village. As poor Dick was not old enough to work, he was very badly off; he got but little for his dinner, and sometimes nothing at all for his breakfast, for the people who lived in the village were very poor indeed, and could not spare much more than the parings of potatoes, and now and then a hard crust of bread.

For all this Dick Whittington was a very sharp boy and was always listening to what everybody talked about. On Sunday he was sure to get near the farmers, as they sat talking on the tombstones in the churchyard, before the parson was come; and once a week you might see little Dick leaning against the signpost of the village alehouse, where people stopped to drink as they came from the next market town; and when the barber's shop door was open, Dick listened to all the news that his customers told one another.

In this manner Dick heard a great many things about the great city called London, for the foolish country people at that time thought that folks in London were all fine gentlemen and ladies and that there was singing and music there all day long and that the streets were all paved with gold.

One day a large wagon and eight horses, all with bells at their heads drove through the village where Dick was standing by the signpost. He thought that this wagon must be going to the fine town of London; so he took courage and asked the wagoneer to let him walk with him by the side of the wagon. As soon as the wagoneer heard that poor Dick had no father or mother, and saw by his ragged clothes that he could not be worse off than he was, he told him he might go if he would, so they set off together.

I could never find out how little Dick contrived to get meat and drink on the road; nor how he could walk so far, for it was a long way, nor what he did at night for a place to lie down to sleep in. Perhaps some good natured people in the towns that he passed through, when they saw he was a poor little ragged boy, gave him something to eat; and perhaps the wagoneer let him get into the wagon at night and take a nap upon one of the boxes or large parcels in the wagon.

Dick, however, got safe to London, and was in such a hurry to see the fine streets paved all over with gold, that I am afraid he did not even stay to thank the kind wagoneer, but ran off as fast as his legs would carry him, through many of the streets, thinking every moment to come to those that were paved with gold, for Dick had seen a guinea hen three times in his own little village and remembered what a deal of money it scratched up in change; so he thought he had nothing to do but to take up some little bits of the pavement and should then have as much money as he could wish for.

Poor Dick ran till he was tired, and had quite forgot his friend the wagoneer; but at last, finding it grow dark, and that every way he turned he saw nothing but dirt instead of gold, he sat down in a dark corner and cried himself to sleep.

Little Dick was all night in the streets; and next morning, being very hungry, he got up and walked about, and asked everybody he met to give him a halfpenny to keep him from starving; but nobody stayed to answer him, and only two or three gave him a halfpenny, so that the poor boy was soon quite weak and faint for the want of victuals.

At last a good natured looking gentleman saw how hungry he looked. "Why don't you go to work, my lad?" said he to Dick. "That I would, but I do not know how to get any," answered Dick.

"If you are willing, come along with me," said the gentleman, and took him to a hayfield, where Dick worked briskly, and lived merrily till the hay was made.

After this he found himself as badly off as before; and being almost starved again, he laid himself down at the door of Mr. Fitzwarren, a rich merchant. Here he was soon seen by the cookmaid, who was an ill-tempered creature, and happened just then to be very busy dressing dinner for her master and mistress. So she called out to poor Dick: "What business have you there, you lazy rogue? There is nothing else but beggars; if you do not take yourself away, we will see how you will like a sousing of some dishwater; I have some here hot enough to make you jump."

Just at that time Mr. Fitzwarren himself came home to dinner; and when he saw a dirty ragged boy lying at the door, he said to him: "Why do you lay there, my boy? You seem old enough to work; I am afraid you are inclined to be lazy."

"No, indeed, sir," said Dick to him, "that is not the case, for I would work with all my heart, but I do not know anybody, and I believe I am very sick for the want of food."

"Poor fellow, get up; let me see what ails you."

Dick now tried to rise, but was obliged to lie down again, being too weak to stand, for he had not eaten any food for three days, and was no longer able to run about and beg a halfpenny of people in the street. So the kind merchant ordered him to be taken into the house, and have a good dinner given him, and be kept to do what dirty work he was able for the cook.

Little Dick would have lived very happy in this good family if it had not been for the ill-natured cook, who was finding fault and scolding him from morning to night, and besides, she was so fond of basting, that when she had no meat to baste, she would baste poor Dick's head and shoulders with a broom, or anything else that happened to fall in her way. At last her ill-usage of him was told to Alice, Mr. Fitzwarren's daughter, who told the cook she should be turned away if she did not treat him kinder.

The ill humor of the cook was now a little amended, but besides this Dick had another hardship to get over. His bed stood in a garret, where there were so many holes in the floor and the walls that every night he was tormented with rats and mice. A gentleman having given Dick a penny for cleaning his shoes, he thought he would buy a cat with it. The next day he saw a girl with a cat, and asked her if she would let him have it for a penny. The girl said she would, and at the same time told him the cat was an excellent mouser.

Dick hid his cat in the garret and always took care to carry a part of his dinner to her; and in a short time he had no more trouble with the rats and mice but slept quite sound every night.

Soon after this his master had a ship ready to sail and as he thought it right that all his servants should have some chance for good fortune as well as himself, he called them all into the parlor and asked them what they would send out for trade.

They all had something that they were willing to venture except poor Dick, who had neither money nor goods, and therefore could send nothing.

For this reason he did not come into the parlor with the rest; but Miss Alice guessed what was the matter and ordered him to be called in. She then said she would lay down some money for him, from her own purse; but the father told her this would not do, for it must be something of Dick's own.

When poor Dick heard this, he said he had nothing but a cat which he bought for a penny some time since of a little girl.

"Fetch your cat then, my good boy," said Mr. Fitzwarren, "and let her go."

Dick went upstairs and brought down poor puss, with tears in his eyes, and gave her to the captain, for he said he should be kept awake again by the rats and mice.

All the company laughed at Dick's odd venture; and Miss Alice, who felt pity for the poor boy, gave him some money to buy another cat.

This, and many other marks of kindness shown him by Miss Alice, made the ill-tempered cook jealous of poor Dick, and she began to use him more cruelly than ever, and always made game of him for sending his cat to sea. She asked him if he thought his cat would sell for as much money as would buy a stick to beat him.

At last poor Dick could not bear this usage any longer, and he thought he would run away from his place; so he packed up his few things, and started very early in the morning, on Allhallows Day, which is the first of November. He walked as far as Holloway; and there he sat down on a stone, which to this day is called Whittington's stone, and began to think to himself which road he should take as he proceeded onwards.

While he was thinking what he should do, the bells of Bow Church, which at that time had only six, began to ring, and he fancied their sound seemed to say to him:

Turn again, Whittington,
Lord Mayor of London.

"Lord Mayor of London!" said he to himself. "Why, to be sure, I would put up with almost anything now, to be Lord Mayor of London, and ride in a fine coach, when I grow to be a man! Well, I will go back, and think nothing of the cuffing and scolding of the old cook, if I am to be Lord Mayor of London at last."

Dick went back and was lucky enough to get into the house, and set about his work, before the old cook came downstairs.

The ship, with the cat on board, was a long time at sea; and was at last driven by the winds on a part of the coast of Barbary, where the only people were the Moors, that the English had never known before.

The people then came in great numbers to see the sailors, who were of different color to themselves, and treated them very civilly, and, when they became better acquainted, were very eager to buy the fine things that the ship was loaded with.

When the captain saw this, he sent patterns of the best things he had to the king of the country, who was so much pleased with them that he sent for the captain to the palace. Here they were placed, as it is the custom of the country, on rich carpets marked with gold and silver flowers. The king and queen were seated at the upper end of the room, and a number of dishes were brought in for dinner. They had not sat long, when a vast number of rats and mice rushed in, helping themselves from almost every dish. The captain wondered at this and asked if these vermin were not very unpleasant.

"Oh yes," said they, "very offensive; and the king would give half his treasure to be freed of them, for they not only destroy his dinner, as you see, but they assault him in his chamber, and even in bed, so that he is obliged to be watched while he is sleeping for fear of them."

The captain jumped for joy; he remembered poor Whittington and his cat, and told the king he had a creature on board the ship that would dispatch all these vermin immediately. The king's head heaved so high at the joy which this news gave him that his turban dropped off his head. "Bring this creature to me," says he. "Vermin are dreadful in a court, and if she will perform what you say, I will load your ship with gold and jewels in exchange for her."

The captain, who knew his business, took this opportunity to set forth the merits of Miss Puss. He told His Majesty that it would be inconvenient to part with her, as, when she was gone, the rats and mice might destroy the goods in the ship—but to oblige His Majesty he would fetch her. "Run, run!" said the queen. "I am impatient to see the dear creature."

Away went the captain to the ship, while another dinner was got ready. He put puss under his arm and arrived at the place soon enough to see the table full of rats.

When the cat saw them, she did not wait for bidding, but jumped out of the captain's arms and in a few minutes laid almost all the rats and mice dead at her feet. The rest of them in their fright scampered away to their holes.

The king and queen were quite charmed to get so easily rid of such plagues and desired that the creature who had done them so great a kindness might be brought to them for inspection. Upon which the captain called: "Pussy, pussy, pussy!" and she came to him. He then presented her to the queen, who started back, and was afraid to touch a creature who had made such a havoc among the rats and mice. However, when the captain stroked the cat and called: "Pussy, pussy," the queen also touched her and cried: "Putty, putty," for she had not learned English. He then put her down on the queen's lap, where she, purring, played with Her Majesty's hand, and then sang herself to sleep.

The king, having seen the exploits of Mrs. Puss, and being informed that she was with young, and would stock the whole country, bargained with the captain for the whole ship's cargo, and then gave him ten times as much for the cat as all the rest amounted to.

The captain then took leave of the royal party, and set sail with a fair wind for England, and after a happy voyage arrived safe in London.

One morning Mr. Fitzwarren had just come to his countinghouse and seated himself at the desk, when somebody came tap, tap, at the door.

"Who's there?" says Mr. Fitzwarren.

"A friend," answered the other. "I come to bring you good news of your ship *Unicorn*."

The merchant, bustling up instantly, opened the door, and who should be seen waiting but the captain and factor, with a cabinet of jewels and a bill of lading, for which the merchant lifted up his eyes and thanked heaven for sending him such a prosperous voyage.

They then told the story of the cat, and showed the rich present that the king and queen had sent for her to poor Dick. As soon as the merchant heard this, he called out to his servants:

"Go fetch him—we will tell him of the same;
Pray call him Mr. Whittington by name."

Mr. Fitzwarren now showed himself to be a good man, for when some of his servants said so great a treasure was too much for Dick, he answered: "God forbid I should deprive him of the value of a single penny."

He then sent for Dick, who at that time was scouring pots for the cook and was quite dirty.

Mr. Fitzwarren ordered a chair be set for him, and so he began to think they were making game of him, at the same time begging them not to play tricks with a poor simple boy but to let him go down again, if they pleased, to his work.

"Indeed, Mr. Whittington," said the merchant, "we are all quite in earnest with you, and I most heartily rejoice in the news these gentlemen have brought you, for the captain has sold your cat to the King of Barbary, and brought you in return for her more riches than I possess in the whole world, and I wish you may long enjoy them!"

Mr. Fitzwarren then told the men to open the great treasure they had brought with them and said: "Mr. Whittington has nothing to do but to put it in some place of safety."

Poor Dick hardly knew how to behave himself for joy. He begged his master to take what part of it he pleased, since he owed it all to his kindness. "No, no," answered Mr. Fitzwarren, "this is all your own, and I have no doubt but you will use it well."

Dick next asked his mistress, and then Miss Alice, to accept a part of his good fortune, but they would not and at the same time told him they felt great joy at his good success. But this poor fellow was too kind-hearted to keep it all to himself; so he made a present to the captain, the mate, and the rest of Mr. Fitzwarren's servants, and even to the ill natured old cook.

After this Mr. Fitzwarren advised him to send for a proper trades-man and get himself dressed like a gentleman; and told him he was welcome to live in his house till he could provide himself with a better.

When Whittington's face was washed, his hair curled, his hat cocked, and he was dressed in a nice suit of clothes, he was as handsome and genteel as any young man who visited at Mr. Fitzwarren's, so that Miss Alice, who had once been so kind to him and thought of him with pity, now looked upon him as fit to be her sweetheart, and the more so, no doubt, because Whittington was now always thinking what he could do to oblige her and making her the prettiest presents that could be.

Mr. Fitzwarren soon saw their love for each other and proposed to join them in marriage; and to this they both readily agreed. A day for the wedding was soon fixed, and they were attended to church by the Lord Mayor, the court of aldermen, the sheriffs, and a great number of the richest merchants in London, whom they afterwards treated with a very rich feast.

History tells us that Mr. Whittington and his lady lived in great splendor and were very happy. They had several children. He was Sheriff of London, also Mayor, and received the honor of knighthood by Henry V.

The figure of Sir Richard Whittington with his cat in his arms, carved in stone, was to be seen till the year 1780 over the archway of the old prison of Newgate that stood across Newgate Street.

How Raja Rasâlu Played Chaupur With King Sarkap
[INDIA]

Raja Rasâlu has been called "the chief legendary hero of the Punjab," and he appears in a cycle of folk narratives.

Now, when evening came, Raja Rasâlu went forth to play *chaupur* with King Sarkap, and as he passed some potters' kilns he saw a cat wandering about restlessly, so he asked what ailed her that she never stood still, and she replied, "My kittens are in an unbaked pot in the kiln yonder. It has just been set alight, and my children will be baked alive; therefore, I cannot rest!"

Her words moved the heart of Raja Rasâlu, and, going to the potter, he asked him to sell the kiln as it was; but the potter replied that he could not settle a fair price till the pots were burnt, as he could not tell how many would come out whole. Nevertheless, after some bargaining, he consented at last to sell the kiln, and Rasâlu, having searched through all the pots, restored the kittens to their mother, and she, in gratitude for his

75

mercy, gave him one of them, saying, "Put it in your pocket, for it will help you when you are in difficulties."

So Raja Rasâlu put the kitten in his pocket, and went to play *chaupur* with the King.

Now, before they sat down to play, Raja Sarkap fixed his stakes. On the first game, his kingdom; on the second, the wealth of the whole world; and on the third, his own head. So, likewise, Raja Rasâlu fixed his stakes. On the first game, his arms; on the second, his horse; and on the third, his own head.

Then they began to play, and it fell to Rasâlu's lot to make the first move. Now he played with the dice given him by Raja Sarkap; then, in addition, Sarkap let loose his famous rat, Dhol Raja, and it ran about the board, upsetting the *chaupur* pieces on the sly, so that Rasâlu lost the first game, and gave up his shining armor.

So the second game began, and once more Dhol Raja, the rat, upset the pieces; and Rasâlu, losing the game, gave up his faithful steed, Bhaunr Irâqi. Then Bhaunr Irâqi, who stood by, found voice, and cried to his master:

"I am born of the sea and of gold;
Dear Prince! trust me now as of old.
  I'll carry you far from these wiles—
My flight, all unspurr'd, will be swift as a bird,
  For thousands and thousands of miles!
Or if needs you must stay; ere the next game you play,
  Place your hand in your pocket, I pray!"

Hearing this, Raja Sarkap frowned, and bade his slaves remove Bhaunr Irâqi, since he gave his master advice in the game. Now when the slaves came to lead the faithful steed away, Rasâlu could not refrain from tears, thinking over the long years during which Bhaunr Irâqi had been his companion. But the horse cried out again:

"Weep not, dear Prince! I shall not eat my bread
Of stranger hands, nor to strange stall be led.
Take thy right hand, and place it as I said."

These words roused some recollection in Rasâlu's mind, and, just at this moment, the kitten in his pocket began to struggle. Then his heart rose up once more, and he called boldly to Raja Sarkap, "Leave my horse and arms here for the present. Time enough to take them away when you have won my head!"

Now, Raja Sarkap, seeing Rasâlu's confident bearing, began to be afraid, and ordered all the women of his palace to come forth in their gayest attire and stand before Rasâlu, so as to distract his attention from the game. But he never even looked at them, and, drawing the dice from his pocket, said to Sarkap, "We have played with your dice all this time; now we will play with mine."

Then the kitten went and sat at the window through which the rat Dhol Raja used to come, and the game began.

After a while, Sarkap, seeing Raja Rasâlu was winning, called to his rat, but when Dhol Raja saw the kitten he was afraid, and would not go farther. So Rasâlu won, and took back his arms. Next he played for his horse, and once more Raja Sarkap called for his rat; but Dhol Raja, seeing the kitten keeping watch, was afraid. So Rasâlu won the second stake, and took back Bhaunr Irâqi.

Then Sarkap brought all his skill to bear on the third game, saying:

"Oh molded pieces, favor me today!
For sooth this is a man with whom I play.
No paltry risk—but life and death at stake;
As Sarkap does, so do, for Sarkap's sake!"

But Rasâlu answered back:

"Oh molded pieces, favor me today!
For sooth it is a man with whom I play.
No paltry risk—but life and death at stake;
As Heaven does, so do, for Heaven's sake!"

So they began to play, while the women stood round in a circle, and the kitten watched Dhol Raja from the window. Then Sarkap lost, first his kingdom, then the wealth of the whole world, and lastly his head.

Just then, a servant came in to announce the birth of a daughter to Raja Sarkap, and he, overcome by misfortunes, said, "Kill her at once! for she has been born in an evil moment and has brought her father ill luck!"

But Rasâlu rose up in his shining armor, tenderhearted and strong, saying, "Not so, oh king! She has done no evil. Give me this child to wife; and if you will vow, by all you hold sacred, never again to play *chaupur* for another's head, I will spare yours now!"

Then Sarkap vowed a solemn vow never to play for another's head; and after that he took a fresh mango branch, and the newborn babe, and placing them on a golden dish, gave them to the prince.

Now, as Rasâlu left the palace, carrying with him the newborn babe and the mango branch, he met a band of prisoners, and they called out to him:

"A royal hawk art thou, Oh King! the rest
But timid wildfowl. Grant us our request—
Unloose these chains, and live for ever blest!"

And Raja Rasâlu hearkened to them, and bade King Sarkap set them at liberty.

Then he went to the Mutri Hills, and placed the newborn babe, Kokilân, in an underground palace and planted the mango branch at the door, saying, "In twelve years the mango tree will blossom; then will I return and marry Kokilân."

And after twelve years the mango tree began to flower and Raja Rasâlu married the Princess Kokilân, whom he won from Sarkap when he played *chaupur* with the king.

The Bremen Town-Musicians
[GERMANY]

A certain man had a donkey, which had carried the corn sacks to the mill indefatigably for many a long year, but his strength was going, and he was growing more and more unfit for work. Then his master began to consider how he might best save his keep, but the donkey, seeing that no good wind was blowing, ran away and set out on the road to Bremen.

"There," he thought, "I can surely be a town-musician."

When he had walked some distance, he found a hound lying on the road, gasping like one who had run till he was tired.

"What are you gasping so for, you big fellow?" asked the donkey.

"Ah," replied the hound, "as I am old, and daily grow weaker, and can no longer hunt, my master wanted to kill me, so I took to flight; but now how can I earn my bread?"

"I tell you what," said the donkey, "I am going to Bremen and shall be town-musician there; go with me and engage yourself also as a musician. I will play the lute, and you shall beat the kettledrum."

The hound agreed, and on they went.

Before long they came to a cat, sitting on the path, with a face like three rainy days!

"Now then, old shaver, what has gone askew with you?" asked the donkey.

"Who can be merry when his neck is in danger?" answered the cat. "Because I am now getting old, and my teeth are worn to stumps, and I prefer to sit by the fire and spin rather than hunt about after mice, my mistress wanted to drown me, so I ran away. But now good advice is scarce. Where am I to go?"

"Go with us to Bremen. You understand night music, so you can be a town-musician."

The cat thought well of it and went with them. After this the three fugitives came to a farmyard, where the cock was sitting upon the gate, crowing with all his might.

"Your crow goes through and through one," said the donkey. "What is the matter?"

"I have been foretelling fine weather, because it is the day on which Our Lady washes the Christ Child's little shirts and wants to dry them," said the cock. "But guests are coming for Sunday, so the housewife has no pity, and has told the cook that she intends to eat me in the soup tomorrow, and this evening I am to have my head cut off. Now I am crowing at full pitch while I can."

"Ah, but red-comb," said the donkey, "you had better come away with us. We are going to Bremen; you can find something better than death. You have a good voice, and if we make music together it must have some quality!"

The cock agreed to this plan and all four went on together. They could not, however, reach the city of Bremen in one day, and in the evening they came to a forest where they meant to pass the night. The donkey and the hound laid themselves down under a large tree, the cat and the cock settled themselves in the branches, but the cock flew right to the top, where he was most safe. Before he went to sleep he looked round on all the four sides and thought in the distance he saw a little spark burning. So he called out to his companions that there must be a house not far off, for he saw a light.

The donkey said, "If so, we had better get up and go on, for the shelter here is bad."

The hound thought that a few bones with some meat on would do him good too! So they made their way to the place where the light was and soon saw it shine brighter and grow larger, until they came to a well-lighted robber's house. The donkey, as the biggest, went to the window and looked in.

"What do you see, my grey horse?" asked the cock.

"What do I see?" answered the donkey. "A table covered with good things to eat and drink and robbers sitting at it enjoying themselves."

"That would be the sort of thing for us," said the cock.

"Yes, yes, how I wish we were there!" said the donkey.

Then the animals took counsel together how they should manage to drive away the robbers, and at last they thought of a plan. The donkey was to place himself with his forefeet upon the window ledge, the hound was to jump on the donkey's back, the cat was to climb upon the dog, and lastly the cock was to fly up and perch upon the head of the cat.

When this was done, at a given signal they began to perform their music together: the donkey brayed, the hound barked, the cat mewed, and the cock crowed. Then they burst through the window into the room, so that the glass clattered! At this horrible din, the robbers sprang up, thinking no otherwise than that a ghost had come in and fled in a great fright out into the forest. The four companions now sat down at the table, well content with what was left, and ate as if they were going to fast for a month.

As soon as the four minstrels had done, they put out the light, and each sought for himself a sleeping place according to his nature and to what suited him. The donkey laid himself down upon some straw in the yard, the hound behind the door, the cat upon the hearth near the warm ashes, and the cock perched himself upon a beam of the roof. And being tired with their long walk, they soon went to sleep.

When it was past midnight and the robbers saw from afar that the light was no longer burning in their house, and all appeared quiet, the captain said, "We ought not to have let ourselves be frightened out of our wits," and ordered one of them to go and examine the house.

The messenger, finding all still, went into the kitchen to light a candle, and, taking the glistening fiery eyes of the cat for live coals, he held a lucifer match to them to light it. But the cat did not understand the joke and flew in his face, spitting and scratching. He was dreadfully frightened and ran to the back door, but the dog, who lay there, sprang up and bit his leg; and as he ran across the yard by the straw heap, the donkey gave him a smart kick with its hind foot. The cock, too, who had been awakened by the noise and had become lively, cried down from the beam, "Cock-a-doodle-doo!"

Then the robber ran back as fast as he could to his captain and said, "Ah, there is a horrible witch sitting in the house, who spat on me and scratched my face with her long claws; and by the door stands a man with a knife, who stabbed me in the leg; and in the yard there lies a black monster, who beat me with a wooden club; and above, upon the roof, sits the judge, who called out, 'Bring the rogue here to me' so I got away as best I could."

After this the robbers did not trust themselves in the house again. But it suited the four musicians of Bremen so well that they did not care to leave it anymore.

And the mouth of him who has told this story is still warm.

The Cat and the Two Sorceresses
[FRANCE]

Once there was a young girl, pretty and wise, who had a stepmother who wished her no good. She was called Annaïc. Her father loved her, but his wife did all that she could to make him detest his daughter also. She went, one day, to find her sister, who was a sorceress, and asked her advice about getting rid of Annaïc.

"Tell her father," suggested the sorceress, "that she leads a scandalous life and he'll throw her out."

But the father would not believe all the evil which was said about his daughter, and the stepmother returned to consult her sister, the sorceress.

"Well," said she this time, "here's a cake which I made which you must make the girl eat; as soon as she's eaten it, her stomach will swell up like that of a pregnant woman, and then the father will have to believe what you tell him about the immoral conduct of his daughter."

The wicked woman returned with the cake of the sorceress and, giving it to Annaïc, said to her:

"Here, my child, eat this honey-cake which I made myself especially for you."

Annaïc took the cake and ate it, without objection and with pleasure, persuaded that this was finally a sign of her stepmother's affection. But, soon enough, her stomach swelled up such that everybody who saw her believed her pregnant, and the poor girl was totally shamed and did not know what to think.

"I warned you," the stepmother then triumphantly said to the father, "that your daughter was behaving badly; now see what a state she's in."

Then the father put Annaïc in a cask and set it out to sea to the mercy of God. The cask broke to pieces on some great rocks. Annaïc got out, without injury, and found herself on an arid island which she believed to be deserted. She withdrew into an underground cave hollowed out in the cliff and, astonished, found there a little room, fully furnished with a bed, several vases of rough-hewn pottery, and a fire in the hearth. She thought that this must be inhabited; but, after having waited a long time until no one appeared, she lay down on the bed and peacefully slept.

Next morning, upon awakening, she found herself still alone. She got up and went to look for shellfish among the rocks for her breakfast; then, all day, she traversed the island and encountered neither a dwelling nor a human being. In the evening she returned to her cave and slept peacefully again. And so the days proceeded.

When her time came, she gave birth to ... a little cat! Great was her sorrow when she saw the creature which she had brought into the world, but she resigned herself, saying:

"Since it's the will of God!"

And she raised and took care of her little cat as she would have a child.

One day, as she sorrowed for her lot and wept, she was astonished to hear the cat speak in the language of humans, to this effect:

"Console yourself, mother, I'll take care of you in my turn and never let you be in want of anything."

And the cat took a sack, which he found in a corner of the cave, put it over his shoulder, and left. He made his way over the whole island, found a castle, and entered it. The residents of this castle were very surprised to see a cat which walked on its two hind legs and carried a sack on its shoulder. He asked for bread, for meat and for wine, and no one thought to refuse him because this was such a strange happening. They filled his sack and off he went. He came back again to the castle every other day, and each time he returned with his sack empty, and in her cave his mother wanted for nothing.

One day the young man of the castle got into an argument while on a pilgrimage, and, having lost his passport, was put in jail. At the castle everybody was desolate, and when the cat came there, according to his custom, he asked about the cause of the sadness and the sorrow which he noticed. They acquainted him with the reason; then he replenished his sack as usual and left. Arriving at the cave, he said to his mother:

"Sorrow and sadness reign at the castle."

"Why is that?"

"The young lord got into a fight while he was on a pilgrimage; he lost his passport and they put him in prison; but I'm going to find him tomorrow in the jail, and I'm going to say to him that if he marries my mother, I'll retrieve his passport and get it back to him."

"Whatever makes you think that he would ever agree to take me as his wife, my child?"

"He might, mother; let me try."

The next day the cat showed up at the prison and asked to speak to the young lord. But the jailer grabbed a broom and chased him out with it. In the face of this assault the cat hopped aside and, seizing an opening, clambered up the wall and entered the prison through a window and said to the prisoner:

"My good lord, you have fed us, my mother and me, since we came to your island, and, in recognition of this kind service, I shall get out of this prison and make to recover your passport—if you will promise to marry my mother."

"How is it, poor beast, that you can speak?" asked the lord, astonished.

"I can speak, and I am not what you think; but, tell me, are you willing to marry my mother?"

"Marry a cat? Me, a Christian? How can you make me such a proposition?"

"Marry my mother and you won't regret it, I tell you. I'll leave you until tomorrow to think about it; I'll come back tomorrow."

And so he left.

The next day he returned with the passport of the young lord and said to him as he held it up:

"Here is your passport; promise me that you'll marry my mother and I'll return it to you; what's more, I'll restore your freedom at once."

The prisoner promised and he got his freedom.

Now, the cat's mother had a sorceress godmother who knew quite well what was happening. She came to find Annaïc, while the cat was away, and spoke to her like this:

"His passport has been returned to the young lord, who has promised to marry you. When the cat returns, take a knife and cut open his stomach. Don't hesitate, because he will immediately be turned into a fine prince and you into a princess of marvellous beauty. Then you will marry the young lord and I will send you fifty handsome knights to attend you night and day."

When the cat returned, his mother sliced open his stomach. Immediately a fine prince, magnificently adorned, emerged from his skin, and she herself became a princess of marvellous beauty. The fifty knights arrived also, and a beautiful, solid-gold carriage came down from the sky. The prince and princess got in and returned to the castle, accompanied by the fifty knights.

The young lord, who was at his window, was mightily astonished to see such a sight, which he couldn't comprehend at all. But he was eager to go down to meet them. The prince moved forward to meet him, taking the princess by the hand, and presented her in these terms:

"Here is my mother, whom you promised to marry; how do you like her?"

The young lord was so troubled and upset by all that he saw and heard that he was speechless and could only stammer these words:

"God, what a beautiful princess...! Yes, certainly...! How is this...? Honored...!"

The marriage was celebrated at once. During the nuptial feast, one could hear, without seeing anyone play, a ravishing music such as is only heard in Heaven. It was the godmother of the new bride, the sorceress, who sent invisible musicians. She had also sent her beautiful gold carriage and now said:

"You only have to go *psit* and my enchanted knights will lift you up into the air and carry you where you wish. But if you return to your father, be very careful when you embrace your stepmother; as for your father, do whatever you wish."

They forthwith got into the carriage, which lifted them up above the clouds and carried them straight to Annaïc's father. He recognized his daughter, and showed great joy at her return, and embraced her tenderly. The stepmother was furious; nevertheless, she pretended, the wretch, that she wished to be embraced too. But the prince cried out to her:

"Hold on, you! You won't embrace my mother; but you'll be recompensed according to your merits."

And they lit a great bonfire and hurled the stepmother and her daughter and also the sorceress onto it.

Then, after eight whole days, there were great celebrations, with entertainments of all sorts, with music, dances and grand parties every day.

Catskin
[ENGLAND]

Once upon a time there was a little girl who, when she came into the world, found she was not wanted there, for her father had long wished for a son and heir, and when a daughter was born instead, he fell into a blind rage and said, "She sha'n't stay long in my house."

Her mother became very sad at this and, fearing her father's hatred, sent away the poor little babe to a foster nurse, who lived in a house by a great oak wood. There the child lived till she was fifteen summers old. Then her old foster mother died, but before she died, she told the poor child at her bedside to hide all her pretty white frocks in the wood by the crystal waterfall that sounded there all day long among the oak trees. Then she was to put on a dress of catskin the old dame gave her and go and seek a place as a servant-maid far away in the town.

Catskin (for so she must now be called) did as the old dame had told her and presently set off all alone in her travels. She wandered a long way and at last came to the town and to a great house. There she knocked at the gate and begged the porter for a place as a servant. He sent her upstairs then to the lady of the house, who looked hard at poor

Catskin and patted her on the head and ended by saying:

"I'm sorry I've no better place for you, my dear, but you can be a scullion under the cook, if you like!"

So Catskin was put under the cook and a very sad life she led with her, for as often as the cook got out of temper, she got a ladle and broke it over poor Catskin's head.

Well, time went on and there was to be a grand ball in the town.

"Oh, Mrs. Cook," said Catskin, "how much I should like to go!"

"You go, with your catskin robe, among the fine ladies and lords, you dirty slut, a very fine figure you'd make!"

And with that she took a basin of water and dashed it in poor Catskin's face.

But Catskin briskly shook her ears and went off to her hiding place in the wood; and there, as an old song says:

> She washed every stain from her skin,
>   In some crystal waterfall;
> Then put on a beautiful dress,
>   And hasted away to the ball.

When she entered, the ladies were mute, overcome by her beauty; but the lord, her young master, at once fell in love with her. He prayed her to be his partner in the dance. To this Catskin said "Yes," and with a sweet smile. All that evening with no other partner but Catskin would he dance.

"Pray tell me, fair maid," he said at last, "where you live."

Now was the sad parting time; but no answer would she give him than this:

> "Kind sir, if the truth I must tell,
> At the sign of the Basin of Water I dwell."

Then Catskin flew from the ballroom and put on her furry robe again and slipt into the kitchen unseen by the cook, who little thought where her scullion had been. The very next day the young squire told his mother he would never rest until he found out this beautiful maid, and who she was, and where she lived.

Well, time went on, and another grand ball was to be given in the town. When Catskin heard of it: "Mrs. Cook, oh, Mrs. Cook," she cried, "how much I should like to go!"

"You go with your catskin robe among the fine lords and ladies, you dirty slut! A very fine figure you'd make!"

And in a great rage she took the ladle and struck poor Catskin's head a terrible blow.

But off went Catskin, none the worse, shaking her ears, and swift to her forest she fled. And there, as the old song says:

> She washed every bloodstain off,
>   In some crystal waterfall;
> Put on a more beautiful dress,
>   And hasted away to the ball.

Now at the ballroom door the young squire was in waiting; he longed to see nothing so much as the beautiful Catskin again. When she arrived he asked her to dance and again she said "Yes" with the same smiling look as before.

And again all the night he would have none but pretty Catskin for his partner.

"Pray tell me," said he, presently, "where you live," for now the time came for parting.

But Catskin no other answer would give him than:

> "Kind sir, if the truth I must tell,
> At the sign of the Broken Ladle I dwell."

Then she flew from the ball, put on her catskin robe under the dark oak trees, and slipt back into the kitchen unseen by the cook, who little thought where she had been.

But now the grandest ball of the whole year was to be held in the town. And just as she had done before, when Catskin heard of it, she resolved that go she must, Mrs. Cook or no Mrs. Cook.

"Mrs. Cook," said Catskin to her one evening, "have you heard of the grand ball? How much I should like to go!"

"You go?" said Mistress Cook as before, "with your catskin robe, you impudent girl! among the fine ladies and lords, a very fine figure you'd cut."

In a fury she snatched up the skimmer and broke it on Catskin's head; but heart-whole and as lively as ever, away to the oakwood Catskin flew; and there, as the song says:

She washed the stains of blood,
  In the crystal waterfall;
Then put on her most beautiful dress,
  And hastened away to the ball.

At the ballroom door the young squire stood waiting, dressed in a velvet coat. He longed to see nothing so much as the beautiful Catskin again. When he asked her to dance, she agreed with a smile, and again, all the night long, with none but fair Catskin would he dance.

"Pray tell me, fair maid, where you live," he said when the parting time came; but she had no other answer for him than this:

"Kind sir, if the truth I must tell,
At the sign of the Broken Skimmer I dwell."

Then she flew from the ball to the oakwood and threw on her catskin cloak again. She slipt into the house unseen by the cook, but not unseen by the young squire, for this time he had followed too fast, and hid himself in the forest, and saw the strange disguise she had put on there.

Next day he took to his bed and sent for the doctor to come and said he should die if Catskin did not come to see him. Well, Catskin was sent for and he told her how dearly he loved her; indeed, if she did not love him, his heart would break.

Then the doctor, who knew how proud the old lady, his mother, was, promised to ask her consent to their wedding. Had she not feared her son would die, her pride would never have yielded; but after a hard struggle she said "Yes!"

The sick young squire got quickly well when he heard the good tidings. And so it was Catskin, before a twelve-month was gone, when the oakwood grew green again, was married to him, and they lived happily foreverafter.

The Legendary Cat

LEGENDS ARE ORAL STORIES told as true (or as *possibly* true or once or sometimes *thought* to be true) by those who spin them. They are "historical," though not by the standards of the historian, or—when the events recounted are said to be recent—they are "the news," though not by the standards of the journalist. Legendary narratives usually are accounts of remarkable, sometimes frightening events—of heroic kings, ghostly apparitions, or strange twists of fate.

In legends, cats assume their powerfully disquieting guise, as consorts of the supernatural and frontmen for the powers of darkness. Witches commonly transform themselves into cats to slink abroad, and various kinds of devils and demons appear in cat form. Faithful cats may save their humans (as in one Japanese story), or sometimes the witch (like those of the San Lorenzo cloister in Florence) may be safely tamed into a kind of domestic truce, but these are the exceptions.

Cats also pop up in those "modern" or "urban" legends which pervade our contemporary world—stories of bizarre, sometimes ironic happenings which supposedly have transpired somewhere on the edges of our everyday lives. Several such tales are included here, beginning with "Who Let the Cat Out of the Bag in Austin, Texas"—actually a short story by Diane Rutt which gives us not only the legend but a lovingly recreated, if fictional, account of its telling. In these stories the emphasis is upon an ironic or even sardonic humor, but the preponderance of dead (or, in one case, disappearing) cats may give cat fanciers pause and make us wonder what such legends say about the society in which we live.

The Witch Cat
[UNITED STATES (Indiana)]

My aunt had a guy who wanted to go with her, but she wouldn't have any dates with him because she'd heard he was a witch.

She woke up in bed one night with a black cat over her face, so she grabbed the cat's foot and bit it. A couple of days later she saw the man with his hand bandaged up.

She said, "Bill, what is the matter with your hand?"

He said, "Oh, I hurt it."

She said that was right where she had bit the cat, and she told him, "I bit it," and he never denied it.

The Baldheaded Cat of Kowashi
[JAPAN]

Kowashi Kamon was a low-rank samurai in the service of the Kyōgoku family in the province of Sanuki. He had an old mother who was eighty years old, and they lived a simple but happy life together in a respectable house.

In the meantime, however, Kowashi noticed some unusual things about his mother. In spite of her crazy teeth she now preferred to eat everything hard and she developed a great relish for fish, to which she had hitherto had a strong aversion, even crunching the bones with great gusto. This made her son wonder, and his wonder waxed greater when late one night he saw her, with her head covered with a handkerchief, dancing a curious dance on the verandah apparently with some invisible companions.

One bright moonlight night a few months later a benighted fish-monger was climbing the mountain pass in the neighborhood on his way home from his peddling when he was suddenly attacked by an army of cats which coveted the fish that remained unsold in his basket. But he drove them away wielding the pole he used for carrying the basket on his shoulder.

Then, seeing that they were no match for him, one of the cats called out to its fellows, "Go and fetch the old woman of Kowashi."

The man, knowing as he did who the old woman was, thought it very strange, and quickly climbing up a nearby pine tree, waited fully prepared for the worst that might come. Presently, the army of cats that were helplessly watching him from a distance, exclaimed, looking down the pass, "Oh, there comes the old woman of Kowashi."

It was an old and big cat with grey fur. She climbed up the same tree and pressed hard upon the fishmonger inch by inch, with her eyes glaring like lanterns and her claws as sharp as knives. This was a tough customer to deal with, thought he, but then, watching for a chance, he dealt the animal a severe blow on the brow with a hook he happened to have about him.

The eastern sky was now turning grey and the whole host of cats dispersed in all directions. The fishmonger jumped down from the tree and, hurrying down the pass, went straight to the house of Kowashi to whom he told all that had happened.

"Ah, I see it all now," said Kowashi Kamon, slapping his thigh, and then whispering to the visitor. "This morning I noticed a scar on my mother's forehead. She says it was caused by stumbling over a stone in the garden last night, but that is doubtful."

Ascertaining, on close examination, that the wound was a stab, he killed the old woman with one stroke of his sword, and there lay instead a big old cat weltering in a pool of blood. Under the floor were discovered the remains of his real mother, reduced to a skeleton.

The Cats of San Lorenzo
[ITALY]

*I*n the cloisters of San Lorenzo there are many cats, and every evening people may be seen who go there to feed them, among whom are many old men and women. But these cats were long ago themselves human, that is to say they were once all wizards and witches, who bear their present form for punishment of an evil deed.

There was once a very wealthy and powerful family in Florence, at the head of which was a gentleman and lady who had an only daughter, in whom was all their love and hope. Among their servants in a higher position was an old woman, who was very vindictive and easily offended, so that she could brood over deadly revenge for years for the least affront, and she fancied she had a great many, because when she had neglected her duty at times she had been scolded by her mistress or master.

Now this old woman knew that death or disaster to the daughter would drive the parents mad; and so having recourse to witchcraft, she put into the drink of the young lady a decoction, the result of which was that she began to waste away, growing weaker and paler, without feeling any pain.

Then her parents, in great fear, consulted the best physicians, who did no good, for indeed it was a case beyond their skill. And at last, beginning to believe that there was something unearthly in it all, they sent for an old woman who cured by occult art. And when she came she looked steadily at the girl, then frowned and shook her head, and asked for a ribbon or cord, no matter what, so that it were one which the young lady had worn about her waist. With this she measured accurately the height of the patient from head to foot, and then the width from hand to hand, it being desirous that the arms be of equal length; but there was the disproportion of the thickness of a piece of money. Then the witch said:

"This is none of my affair as regards the cure. Your daughter is bewitched, and I can indeed make the witch appear, but to beat her and compel her to remove the spell depends on you alone."

Now they, suspecting the old servant, sent for her, but she had disappeared and could not be found. Then the doctress took a caldron, and put into it hot water and the undergarments of the girl and certain herbs, and boiled them all together, singing an incantation, and, taking a knife, sharpened it on the table, whetting it on the chemise of the young lady.

Then the old servant woman appeared at the door, against her will, forced by the power of the spell, in an agony of rage and bitterness; but she was at once seized and beaten, whereupon she consented to unbewitch the girl, who speedily recovered.

Now Florence was at that time fearfully afflicted with evil witches, who defied all authority and spread disease and death far and wide; but this affair of the bewitched lady being made known, both priests and laymen rose up in wrath, and the sorceress fled for sanctuary to the cloisters of San Lorenzo.

Then to save their lives the *strege* [witches] made a compromise with the priests, and it was agreed that they should no longer live as witches, or do any harm, but all live and die as cats in the cloister, where they should be regularly fed, and exist in peace. Which agreement has been duly carried out to this day, and among these cats are many who were once witches in human form hundreds of years ago.

The Vampire Cat of Nabéshima
[JAPAN]

Here is a tradition in the Nabéshima family (the family of the Prince of Hizen) that, many years ago, the prince was bewitched and cursed by a cat that had been kept by one of his retainers. This prince had in his house a lady of rare beauty, called O Toyo; amongst all his ladies she was the favorite, and there was none who could rival her charms and accomplishments. One day the prince went out into the garden with O Toyo and remained enjoying the fragrance of the flowers until sunset, when they returned to the palace, never noticing that they were being followed by a large cat. Having parted with her lord, O Toyo retired to her own room and went to bed. At midnight she awoke with a start, and became aware of a huge cat that crouched watching her; and when she cried out, the beast sprang on her, and, fixing its cruel teeth in her delicate throat, throttled her to death. What a piteous end for so fair a dame, the darling of her prince's heart, to die suddenly, bitten to death by a cat! Then the cat, having scratched out a grave under the verandah, buried the corpse of O Toyo and, assuming her form, began to bewitch the prince.

But my lord the prince knew nothing of all this, and little thought that the beautiful creature who caressed and fondled him was an impish and foul beast that had slain his mistress and assumed her shape in order to drain out his life's blood. Day by day, as time went on, the prince's strength dwindled away; the color of his face was changed, and became pale and livid; and he was as a man suffering from a deadly sickness. Seeing this, his councillors and his wife became greatly alarmed; so they summoned the physicians, who prescribed various remedies for him; but the more medicine he took, the more serious did his illness appear, and no treatment was of any avail. But most of all did he suffer in the nighttime, when his sleep would be troubled and disturbed by hideous dreams. In consequence of this, his councillors nightly appointed a hundred of his retainers to sit up and watch over him; but, strange to say, towards ten o'clock on the very first night that the watch was set, the guards were seized with a sudden and unaccountable drowsiness, which they could not resist, until one by one every man had fallen asleep. Then the false O Toyo came in and harassed the prince until morning. The following night the same thing occurred, and the prince was subjected to the imp's tyranny, while his guards slept helplessly around him. Night after night this was repeated, until at last three of the prince's councillors determined themselves to sit up on guard, and see whether they could overcome this mysterious drowsiness; but they fared no better than the others, and by ten o'clock were fast asleep.

The next day the three councillors held a solemn conclave, and their chief, one Isahaya Buzen, said:

"This is a marvellous thing, that a guard of a hundred men should thus be overcome by sleep. Of a surety, the spell that is upon my lord and upon his guard must be the work of witchcraft. Now, as all our efforts are of no avail, let us seek out Ruiten, the chief priest of the temple called Miyô In, and beseech him to put up prayers for the recovery of my lord."

And the other councillors' approving of what Buzen had said, they went to the priest Ruiten and engaged him to recite litanies that the prince might be restored to health.

So it came to pass that Ruiten, the chief priest of Miyô In, offered up prayers nightly for the prince. One night, at the ninth hour (midnight), when he had finished his religious exercises and was preparing to lie down to sleep, he fancied that he heard a noise outside in the garden, as if someone were washing himself at the well. Deeming this passing strange, he looked down from the window; and there in the moonlight he saw a handsome young soldier, some twenty-four years of age, washing himself. When he had finished cleaning himself and had put on his clothes, he stood before the figure of Buddha and prayed fervently for the recovery of my lord the prince. Ruiten looked on with admiration; and the young man, when he had made an end of his prayer, was going away; but the priest stopped him, calling out to him:

"Sir, I pray you to tarry a little; I have something to say to you."

"At your reverence's service. What may you please to want?"

"Pray be so good as to step up here and have a little talk."

"By your reverence's leave."

And with this he went upstairs.

Then Ruiten said: "Sir, I cannot conceal my admiration that you, being so young a man, should have so loyal a spirit. I am Ruiten, the chief priest of this temple, who am engaged in praying for the recovery of my lord. Pray what is your name?"

"My name, sir, is Itô Sôda, and I am serving in the infantry of Nabéshima. Since my lord has been sick, my one desire has been to assist in nursing him; but, being only a simple soldier, I am not of sufficient rank to come into his presence, so I have no resource but to pray to the gods of the country and to Buddha that my lord may regain his health."

When Ruiten heard this, he shed tears in admiration of the fidelity of Itô Sôda and said:

"Your purpose is, indeed, a good one; but what a strange sickness this is that my lord is afflicted with! Every night he suffers from horrible dreams; and the retainers who sit up with him are all seized with a mysterious sleep, so that not one can keep awake. It is very wonderful."

"Yes," replied Sôda, after a moment's reflection, "this certainly must be witchcraft. If I could but obtain leave to sit up one night with the prince, I would fain see whether I could not resist this drowsiness and detect the goblin."

At last the priest said, "I am in relations of friendship with Isahaya Buzen, the chief councillor of the prince. I will speak to him of you and of your loyalty, and will intercede with him that you may attain your wish."

"Indeed, sir, I am most thankful. I am not prompted by any vain thought of self-advancement. Should I succeed, all I wish for is the recovery of my lord. I commend myself to your kind favor."

"Well, then, tomorrow night I will take you with me to the councillor's house."

"Thank you, sir, and farewell." And so they parted.

On the following evening Itô Sôda returned to the temple Miyô In, and, having found Ruiten, accompanied him to the house of Isahaya Buzen; then the priest, leaving Sôda outside, went in to converse with the councillor, and inquire after the prince's health.

"And pray, sir, how is my lord? Is he in any better condition since I alone have been offering up prayers for him?"

"Indeed, no; his illness is very severe. We are certain he must be the victim of some foul sorcery; but as there are no means of keeping a guard awake after ten o'clock, we cannot catch a sight of the goblin, so we are in the greatest trouble."

"I feel deeply for you: it must be most distressing. However, I have something to tell you. I think that I have found a man who will detect the goblin; and I have brought him with me."

"Indeed! who is the man?"

"Well, he is one of my lord's foot soldiers, named Itô Sôda, a faithful fellow, and I trust that you will grant his request to be permitted to sit up with my lord."

"Certainly, it is wonderful to find so much loyalty and zeal in a common soldier," replied Isahaya Buzen, after a moment's reflection. "Still, it is impossible to allow a man of such low rank to perform the office of watching over my lord."

"It is true that he is but a common soldier," urged the priest, "but why not raise his rank in consideration of his fidelity, and then let him mount guard?"

"It would be time enough to promote him after my lord's recovery. But come, let me see this Itô Sôda, that I may know what manner of man he is; if he pleases me, I will consult with the other councillors, and perhaps we may grant his request."

"I will bring him in forthwith," replied Ruiten, who thereupon went out to fetch the young man.

When he returned, the priest presented Itô Sôda to the councillor, who looked at him attentively, and, being pleased with his comely and gentle appearance, said:

"So I hear that you are anxious to be permitted to mount guard in my lord's room at night. Well, I must consult with the other councillors, and we will see what can be done for you."

When the young soldier heard this he was greatly elated, and took his leave after warmly thanking Ruiten, who had helped him to gain his object. The next day the councillors held a meeting, and sent for Itô Sôda, and told him that he might keep watch with the other retainers that very night. So he went his way in high spirits, and at nightfall, having made all his preparations, took his place among the hundred gentlemen who were on duty in the prince's bedroom.

Now the prince slept in the center of the room, and the hundred guards around him sat keeping themselves awake with entertaining conversation and pleasant conceits. But, as ten o'clock approached, they began to doze off as they sat; and in spite of all their endeavors to keep one another awake, by degrees they all fell asleep. Itô Sôda all this while felt an irresistible desire to sleep creeping over him, and, though he tried by all sorts of ways to rouse himself, he saw that there was no hope for it, but by resorting to an extreme measure, for which he had already made his preparations. Drawing out a piece of oil paper which he had brought with him, and spreading it over the mats, he sat down upon it; then he took the small knife which he carried in the sheath of his dirk, and stuck it into his own thigh. For awhile the pain of the wound kept him awake; but as the slumber by which he was assailed was the work of sorcery, little by little he became drowsy again. Then he twisted the knife round and round in his thigh, so that the pain becoming very violent, he was proof against the feeling of sleepiness, and kept a faithful watch. Now the oil paper which he had spread under his legs was in order to prevent the blood, which might spurt from his wound, from defiling the mats.

So Itô Sôda remained awake, but the rest of the guard slept; and as he watched, suddenly the sliding doors of the prince's room were drawn open, and he saw a figure coming in stealthily, and, as it drew nearer, the form was that of a marvellously beautiful woman some twenty-three years of age. Cautiously she looked around her; and when she saw that all the guard were asleep, she smiled an ominous smile and was going up to the prince's bedside when she perceived that in one corner of the room there was a man yet awake. This seemed to startle her, but she went up to Sôda and said:

"I am not used to seeing you here. Who are you?"

"My name is Itô Sôda, and this is the first night that I have been on guard."

"A troublesome office, truly! Why, here are all the rest of the guard asleep. How is it that you alone are awake? You are a trusty watchman."

"There is nothing to boast about. I'm asleep myself, fast and sound."

"What is that wound on your knee? It is all red with blood."

"Oh! I felt very sleepy; so I stuck my knife into my thigh, and the pain of it has kept me awake."

"What wondrous loyalty!" said the lady.

"Is it not the duty of a retainer to lay down his life for his master? Is such a scratch as this worth thinking about?"

Then the lady went up to the sleeping prince and said, "How fares it with my lord tonight?" But the prince, worn out with sickness, made no reply. But Sôda was watching her eagerly, and guessed that it was O Toyo, and made up his mind that if she attempted to harass the prince he would kill her on the spot. The cat goblin, however, which in the form of O Toyo had been tormenting the prince every night, and had come again that very night for no other purpose, was defeated by the watchfulness of Itô Sôda; for whenever she drew near to the sick man, thinking to put her spells upon him, she would turn and look behind her, and there she saw Itô Sôda glaring at her; so she had no help for it but to go away again, and leave the prince undisturbed.

At last the day broke, and the other officers, when they awoke and opened their eyes, saw that Itô Sôda had kept awake by stabbing himself in the thigh; and they were greatly ashamed, and went home crestfallen.

That morning Itô Sôda went to the house of Isahaya Buzen, and told him all that had occurred the previous night. The councillors were all loud in their praise of Itô Sôda's behavior, and ordered him to keep watch again that night. At the same hour, the false O Toyo came and looked all round the room, and all the guards were asleep, excepting Itô Sôda, who was wide awake; and so, being again frustrated, she returned to her own apartments.

Now as since Sôda had been on guard the prince had passed quiet nights, his sickness began to get better, and there was great joy in the palace, and Sôda was promoted and rewarded with an estate. In the meanwhile O Toyo, seeing that her nightly visits bore no fruits, kept away; and from that time forth the night-guards were no longer subject to fits of drowsiness. This coincidence struck Sôda as very strange, so he went to Isahaya Buzen and told him that of a certainty this O Toyo was no other than a goblin. Isahaya Buzen reflected for awhile, and said:

"Well, then, how shall we kill the foul thing?"

"I will go to the creature's room as if nothing were the matter and try to kill her; but in case she should try to escape, I will beg you to order eight men to stop outside and lie in wait for her."

Having agreed upon this plan, Sôda went at nightfall to O Toyo's apartment, pretending to have been sent with a message from the prince. When she saw him arrive, she said:

"What message have you brought me from my lord?"

"Oh! nothing in particular. Be so good as to look at this letter."

And as he spoke he drew near to her, and, suddenly drawing his dirk, cut at her; but the goblin, springing back, seized a halbred, and glaring fiecely at Sôda, said:

"How dare you behave like this to one of your lord's ladies? I will have you dismissed."

And she tried to strike Sôda with the halbred. But Sôda fought desperately with his dirk; and the goblin, seeing that she was no match for him, threw away the halbred, and from a beautiful woman became suddenly transformed into a cat, which, springing up the sides of the room, jumped onto the roof. Isahaya Buzen and his eight men who were watching outside shot at the cat, but missed it, and the beast made good its escape.

So the cat fled to the mountains and did much mischief among the surrounding people, until at last the Prince of Hizen ordered a great hunt, and the beast was killed.

But the prince recovered from his sickness; and Itô Sôda was richly rewarded.

King Arthur's Fight With the Great Cat
[*CELTIC*]

M
erlin told King Arthur that the people beyond the Lake of Lausanne greatly desired his help, "for there repaireth a devil that destroyeth the country. It is a cat so great and ugly that it is horrible to look on." For one time a fisher came to the lake with his nets, and he promised to give Our Lord the first fish he took. It was a fish worth thirty shillings; and when he saw it so fair and great, he said to himself softly, "God shall not have this; but I will surely give him the next." Now the next was still better, and he said, "Our Lord may yet wait awhile; but the third shall be His without doubt." So he cast his net but drew out only a little kitten as black as any coal.

And when the fisher saw it he said he had need of it at home for rats and mice; and he nourished it and kept it in his house, till it strangled him and his wife and children. Then the cat fled to a high mountain and destroyed and slew all that came in his way and was great and terrible to behold.

When the king heard this he made ready and rode to the Lac de Lausanne and found the country desolate and void of people, for neither man nor woman would inhabit the place for fear of the cat.

And the king was lodged a mile from the mountain, with Sir Gawain and Merlin and others. And they climbed the mountain, Merlin leading the way. And when they were come up, Merlin said to the king, "Sir, in that rock liveth the cat," and he showed him a great cave, large and deep, in the mountain.

"And how shall the cat come out?" said the king.

"That shall ye see hastily," quoth Merlin, "but look you, be ready to defend, for anon he will assail you."

"Then draw ye all back," said the king, "for I will prove his power."

And when they withdrew, Merlin whistled loud, and the cat leaped out of the cave, thinking it was some wild beast, for he was hungry and fasting; and he ran boldly to the king, who was ready with his spear and thought to smite him through the body. But the fiend seized the spear in his mouth and broke it in twain.

Then the king drew his sword, holding his shield also before him. And as the cat leaped at his throat, he struck him so fiercely that the creature fell to the ground but soon was up again and ran at the king so hard that his claws gripped though the hauberk to the flesh, and the red blood followed the claws.

Now the king was nigh falling to earth, but when he saw the red blood he was wonder-wrath, and with his sword in his right hand and his shield at his breast, he ran at the cat vigorously, who sat licking his claws, all wet with blood. But when he saw the king coming towards him, he leapt up to seize him by the throat, as before, and stuck his forefeet so firmly in the shield that they stayed there; and the king smote him on the legs, so that he cut them off to the knees, and the cat fell to the ground.

Then the king ran at him with his sword; but the cat stood on his hind-legs and grinned with his teeth and coveted the throat of the king, and the king tried to smite him on the head; but the cat strained his hinder feet and leaped at the king's breast and fixed his teeth in the flesh, so that the blood streamed down from breast and shoulder.

Then the king struck him fiercely on the body, and the cat fell head downwards, but the feet stayed in the hauberk. And the king smote them asunder, on which the cat fell to the ground, where he howled and brayed so loudly that it was heard through all the king's host, and he began to creep towards the cave; but the king stood between him and the cave and, when he tried to catch the king with his teeth, struck the cat dead.

Then Merlin and the others ran to him and asked how it was with him.

"Well, blessed be Our Lord!" said the king, "for I have slain this devil; but, verily, I never had such a doubt of myself, not even when I slew the giant on the mountain; therefore I thank the Lord."

(This was the great giant of St. Michael's Mount, who supped all the season on seven knave children chopped in a charger of white silver, with powder of precious spices and goblets full plenteous of Portugal wine.)

"Sir," said the barons, "ye have great cause for thankfulness."

Then they looked on the feet that were left in the shield and in the hauberk and said, "Such feet were never seen before!" And they took the shield and showed it to the host with great joy.

So the king let the shield be with the cat's feet; but the other feet he had laid in a coffin to be kept. And the mountain was called from that day The Mountain of the Cat, and the name will never be changed while the world endureth.

The Demon Cat
[IRELAND]

There was a woman in Connemara, the wife of a fisherman. As he had always had good luck, she had plenty of fish at all times stored away in the house ready for market. But, to her great annoyance, she found that a great cat used to come in at night and devour all the best and finest fish. So she kept a big stick by her and determined to watch.

One day, as she and a woman were spinning together, the house suddenly became quite dark; and the door was burst open as if by the blast of the tempest, when in walked a huge black cat, who went straight up to the fire, then turned round and growled at them.

"Why, surely this is the devil," said a young girl who was by, sorting fish.

"I'll teach you to call me names," said the cat; and, jumping at her, he scratched her arm till the blood came. "There now," he said, you will be more civil another time when a gentleman comes to see you."

And, with that, he walked over to the door, and shut it close to prevent any of them going out, for the poor young girl, while crying loudly from fright and pain, had made a desperate rush to get away.

Just then a man was going by, and, hearing the cries, he pushed open the door and tried to get in; but the cat stood on the threshold and would let no one pass. On this the man attacked him with a stick, and gave him a sound blow; the cat, however, was more than a match in the fight, for it flew at him, and tore his face and hands so badly that the man at last took to his heels, and ran away as fast as he could.

"Now, it's time for my dinner," said the cat, going up to examine the fish that was laid out on the tables. "I hope the fish is good today. Now, don't disturb me, or make a fuss; I can help myself."

With that, he jumped up, and began to devour all the best fish, while he growled at the woman.

"Away out of this, you wicked beast!" she cried, giving it a blow with the tongs that would have broken its back, only it was a devil. "Out of this; no fish shall you have today!"

But the cat only grinned at her, and went on tearing and despoiling and devouring the fish, evidently not a bit the worse for the blows. On this both the women attacked it with sticks, and struck hard blows enough to kill it, on which the cat glared at them and spit fire; then, making a leap, it tore their heads and arms till the blood came, and the frightened women rushed shrieking from the house.

But presently the mistress of the house returned, carrying with her a bottle of holy water; and, looking in, she saw the cat still devouring the fish, and not minding. So she crept over quietly, and threw holy water on it without a word. No sooner was this done than a dense, black smoke filled the place, through which nothing was seen but the two red eyes of the cat burning like coals of fire. Then the smoke gradually cleared away, and she saw the body of the creature burning slowly, till it became shrivelled and black like a cinder, and finally disappeared. And from that time the fish remained untouched and safe from harm, for the power of the Evil One was broken, and the Demon Cat was seen no more.

The Story of the Faithful Cat
[JAPAN]

*A*bout sixty years ago, in the summertime, a man went to pay a visit at a certain house in Osaka, and, in the course of conversation, said:

"I have eaten some extraordinary cakes today," and on being asked what he meant, he told the following story:

I received the cakes from the relatives of a family who were celebrating the hundredth anniversary of the death of a cat that had belonged to their ancestors. When I asked the history of the affair, I was told that, in former days, a young girl of the family, when she was about sixteen years old, used always to be followed about by a tomcat, who was reared in the house, so much so that the two were never separated for an instant.

When her father perceived this, he was very angry, thinking that the tomcat, forgetting the kindness with which he had been treated for years in the house, had fallen in love with his daughter, and intended to cast a spell upon her; so he determined that he must kill the beast. As he was planning this in secret, the cat overheard him, and that night went to his pillow and, assuming a human voice, said to him:

"You suspect me of being in love with your daughter; and although you might well be justified in so thinking, your suspicions are groundless. The fact is this: There is a very large old rat who has been living for many years in your granary. Now it is this old rat who is in love with my young mistress, and this is why I dare not leave her side for a moment, for fear the old rat should carry her off. Therefore I pray you to dispel your suspicions. But as I, by myself, am no match for the rat, there is a famous cat, named Buchi, at the house of Mr. So-and-so, at Ajikawa; if you will borrow that cat, we will soon make an end of the old rat."

When the father awoke from his dream, he thought it so wonderful, that he told the household of it; and the following day he got up very early and went off to Ajikawa, to inquire for the house which the cat had indicated, and had no difficulty in finding it; so he called upon the master of the house, and told him what his own cat had said, and how he wished to borrow the cat Buchi for a little while.

"That's a very easy matter to settle," said the other. "Pray take him with you at once."

And, accordingly, the father went home with the cat Buchi in charge. That night he put the two cats into the granary; and after a little while a frightful clatter was heard, and then all was still again; so the people of the house opened the door and crowded out to see what had happened; and there they beheld the two cats and the rat all locked together and panting for breath. So they cut the throat of the rat, which was as big as either of the cats; then they attended to the two cats; but, although they gave them ginseng and other restoratives, they both got weaker and weaker, until at last they died. So the rat was thrown into the river; but the two cats were buried with all honors in a neighboring temple.

Who Let the Cat Out of the Bag in Austin, Texas
[UNITED STATES]

A short story by Diane Rutt

*I*t was like this. You know. I work in this office with a real bunch of lightheads. All they talk about is how to make chuck steak taste like sirloin. I think you understand the kind of yakkin I mean.... Most of the time I just type. Kind of ignorin the gaff goin on around me. But then there is Billie May Jackson. She's in the typists' pool, too. She's also a lighthead. But she's a funny lighthead, and when she gets goin on one of her neighborhood stories, I stand there with the other dummies and laugh my head off....

One morning Billie May comes in with a story that is just too much. Billie May is the typical rodeo type. She wears tight slacks, sits with her legs apart, talks from the side of her mouth, looks you straight in the eye, pointin her finger at you, and when she tells a story, man she lives every minute of it. "Guess what happened to my sister's neighbor," she says cooly. All the girls gather around and in unison they reply, "Okay, what happened to your sister's neighbor?" They wait eagerly for Billie May to go on with the story.

At this point Billie May starts to giggle so hard, throwin her head way back, she can't even talk. Now I'm gettin peeved because I want to get back to work, but how can I until I find out what happened to her sister's neighbor? "Okay," I say, "now that you've got me wantin to know, stop that stupid laughin and *talk!*"

She takes a deep breath and tries again real hard not to laugh. "Well," she begins, "you know this rich old gal I'm always tellin you about." Another deep breath ... giggle....

110

"Well the other mornin she's pullin that new big white Cadillac out of her garage, tryin to be real careful not to scratch the fender, and what does she do?" Chorus: "Okay what does she do?" Billie May answers real quickly. "She backs over a cat and kills it." "Ha ha" I said. "That's really a good story." "Wait a minute, dummy," Billie May says. "Give me a chance to finish.

"This ain't no alley cat. This is one of them fancy dodos. Long gray hair, green eyes, diamond collar. The kind rich folks leave their money to when they die. Even got a special certificate with her name in gold letters, 'Pussy Willow.' Now," says Billie May. "My sister's neighbor knows where this cat resides"—Billie's tryin to be fancy now—"and she also knows that them people that live in that residence, they really dig this cat. She's their baby. So she says to herself, 'I cain't leave this animal here to be picked up by the garbage truck. I'd better go and confess my sin.' So-o, she goes up to the residence of this long grey-haired cat and rings the doorbell. No answer. 'God damn it, nobody is at home,' says she. 'Can I leave this jeweled treasure lyin in the street and ride off without breakin the news to them?' She thinks a while. 'Nope, the best thing to do is to get rid of the cat and then tell 'em (gently as I can).' "

Billie May breathes deeply again and says, "So she goes into her house, gets a paper towel and a big brown sack. She goes back outside, throws the towel over the corpse, picks it up and shoves it into the sack. Then she puts the parcel on the back seat of her car and drives off." After that there is a long pause.

Angrily, I asked her, "That's a story?" "Wait a minute, you nut!" Billie May yells. "Cain't you honor one of woman's best friends by listening to the whole story?" "Okay," I said, "I'll be quiet. Continue."

"All right," continues Billie. "Just picture our killer now drivin this big fancy car, daid cat settin on the back seat, and her drivin herself to the mall.... Oh yeah, I forgot to tell you that she was on her way to some Easter shoppin.

"Well two minutes later she completely forgets about the cat and all she is thinkin about is what she needs to look pretty on Easter Sunday in St. David's Church. She parks her car in that big parkin lot, forgettin about the daid cat. She's wanderin around the Mall, goin from one shop to another, spendin money like it's goin outa style and what does she see?" Another pause.... Chorus: "Okay, what does she see?"

"Well," Billie goes on, "She sees this sorta make-believe farm that they put up for the kids specially for Easter. You know what I'm talkin about. Kinda little zoo with rabbits and chicks and straw for them to lay on. And there's some darlin dark grey soft bunnies, with their eyes closed tight, sleepin, not givin a damn. Whamo! A light turns on in her haid. She grabs all her packages and runs out to the parkin lot. Now she is gettin frantic and starts lookin for the big white Cadillac. She goes up one aisle and down another, tryin to remember where she parked the dern thing.

"Whew, finally she spots it but now hear this ... there is somethin funny goin on out there. Seems like she ain't the only one lookin for a car. She spots this fat dame, real sloppy like, big black coat, big black slacks and of all things, she's wearin white sneakers. She ain't lookin at the outside of the cars, she's lookin on the inside. My sister's neighbor stops right there. She sees her go from car to car, and where does she stop? Right at the white Cadillac. She looks inside and then she looks all around makin sure no one is watchin her (she thinks), opens the door, grabs the paper sack, shoves it under her arm, and walks quickly into the mall. Sooo what does my sister's neighbor and owner of this bundle do? Call the police? Not on your life. This is too exciting. She wants to see what happens when this gal finds out what she stole. So, she turns around and follows right behind. She's followin this dame around a good hour or more and man she's gettin tired. The fat gal goes to Penneys, tries on a pair of shoes, still carryin this daid cat under her arm, goes into the tropical fish store, looks at the little goldfish swimmin around. She even stops and looks at the rabbits and chicks and talks to them cute like. *Finally* she goes into Luby's and decides to eat somethin, still carryin around the brown paper sack. She gets herself a piece of lemon pie and a cup of coffee and finds herself a table near the window. My sister's neighbor ... she does the same. Only she gets cherry pie. Well, they're both sittin there eatin their pie, drinkin coffee. *At last* the gal decides to see what she stole. My sister's neighbor is still watchin her carefully and she's beginnin to get a little nervous. The sack is settin on a chair next to the gal's pocketbook. She stops eatin for a moment, lights a cigarette, and then lookin straight ahead, she slips her right hand into the sack. She turns white and faints dead away. Man, now everyone in Luby's is gettin excited. The manager comes over and he shoos everybody away and he hollers to the cashier, 'Call Brackenridge and get an ambulance out here.' "

At this point, Billie May's voice gets soft. She knows she's got everybody on pins and needles and she continues. "Everybody is crowdin around the fat gal, layin on the floor. They're all whisperin, 'Is she daid? What happened? Maybe she's p.g.' In comes two dudes dressed in white, carryin a stretcher. 'Stand back,' somebody in the crowd hollers. One of the attendants takes out a thingamajig and listens to her heart. 'She's okay,' he says, 'Stand back please.' They gently lift her onto the stretcher, take her purse, put that on the stretcher, and they start to walk out. Someone yells, 'Hey, this package is hers, too!' so the attendant grabs the brown paper sack ... with the cat in it ... lays it on her chest and they carry her out.

"Now," says Billie May, "ain't that a story?"

"Yep," says I, "... that's a story."

The Comic Cat

To THE MODERN URBANITE, folk humor may seem coarse or cruel as well as clever. Certainly in the stories which appear in this section we find misogyny, violence and ill will as well as clever trickery and ironic twists. Yet humor often skirts the edge of human misery and those darker moods we may prefer to otherwise ignore. The tale of "The Lazy Cat," wherein both a cat and her mistress are beaten by the man of the house, may not strike a humorous chord in many readers. Yet it uses a wide-spread folk motif, certainly meant to be comic, which involves the "tam-ing" of a recalcitrant woman via indirection. The tall tale of "The Wooden-Legged Cat" makes light of the infirm. Yet there is no denying the broad humorous appeal of the ultimate triumph of the cat minus one leg.

Some of the other stories in this book are not without humor, but those in this section seem to intend comedy—gentle or cruel—as their very centers. Several are modern jokes and one is a cumulative tale (a type of story in which the teller delights the hearer by invoking an ever-growing chain of things or events). One, the final tale, involves a "cat" rather that a cat but seemed an appropriate inclusion nonetheless, result-ing—like the first tale in the section—in cats' getting an awesome reputa-tion, even if it comes out of stupidity and misunderstanding.

King Cat
[HUNGARY]

Once upon a time there lived a poor widow, who had a big tomcat. Tom was as playful and as fond of titbits as any little kitten. One morning he lapped up all the milk which was kept in the pan. The widow got very angry with him and, having slapped him vigorously, turned him out. The chastised cat thereupon hid at the edge of the village, crouching beside a bridge and moping. At the other end of the bridge sat Reynard, the fox, swinging his bushy tail. The fox became startled, jumped up and spun around. Tom also took fright and recoiled all a-bristle. For a while, they kept staring at each other. Never in his life had Reynard seen a cat, nor had Tom ever caught sight of a fox. Both of them were terrified; neither of them knew what to do next.

Finally it was Reynard who plucked up enough courage to address the cat:

"May I ask without meaning any offense what genteel clan you belong to?"

"I am King of Cats!"

"King of Cats? Never heard of him!"

"Well, you ought to have heard about him. So great is the power I wield that I can reduce any animal to obedience."

Now Reynard got scared indeed and humbly invited Tom to be his guest for a bite of chicken. As it was rather close on noon and our tomcat could have done with something to eat, he didn't wait for the invitation to be repeated, and so they set out for Reynard's den. Tom soon fitted himself into his royal role and much enjoyed the respectful humility with which the fox waited upon him, as if he really were a genuine king. He behaved quite like a lord, speaking little and eating much. Having finished his dinner, he curled up for a nap, first ordering the fox to watch over him and to see that nobody should disturb his dreams.

Reynard obediently took up his post as sentry at the entrance to the den. Just then a little rabbit happened to stroll by.

"Hullo, Bunny!" barked the fox. "Keep off these grounds, for my lord, King Cat, is asleep in there. If he happens to come out you won't know where to run to; so great is the power he wields that he can reduce any animal to obedience!"

The scared little rabbit hopped off to a quiet glade, where he squatted down and began to rack his brains as to who King Cat might be. "Never did I hear of him," he thought.

Master Bruin, too, happened to tramp that way. Bunny asked him politely:

"Where are you walking to, Master Bruin?"

"I felt rather bored and I thought I would take a stroll."

"You better keep off these grounds because Reynard the fox says his lord, King Cat, is asleep in there! If he happens to come out, you won't know where to run to; so great is the power he wields that he can reduce any animal to obedience!"

"King Cat! I never heard of him! Who the devil might he be? Well, I'll go and have a look at him, and see for myself what that King Cat looks like!"

With these words he set off toward Reynard's den.

"Hullo, Master Bruin," said the fox. "Keep off these grounds, for my lord, King Cat, is asleep in there and if he happens to come out, you won't know where to run to; so great is the power he wields that he can reduce any animal to obedience!"

On hearing this Master Bruin lost his courage and, turning his back without uttering a word, returned to Bunny, in whose company he found Uncle Wolf and Sir Crow, airing their grievances, for they too had been turned away.

"Who might he be, this King Cat? We never heard of him!" they all were saying. Thereupon they solemnly considered what to do as to have a look at him. They agreed to invite him to dinner together with the fox, and charged Sir Crow with delivering their invitation.

When Reynard saw Sir Crow approaching, he got very angry with him and gave him a good dressing down for pestering him again.

"Get out of here! Haven't I told you that King Cat is my lord! If he happens to come out, you won't know where to run to; so great is the power he wields that he can reduce any animal to obedience!"

"I know it, I know it very well, and, believe me, I haven't come on my own account, but was sent by Master Bruin, by Uncle Wolf and by

Bunny to invite you to dine with them!"

"Ah, that is different. Wait a moment, please!"

And saying this, Reynard went into the den to report to King Cat. After a while he reappeared and informed Sir Crow that King Cat was pleased to accept the invitation and that the two of them would honor them with their presence; only they must be informed where to go!

"Tomorrow I shall come for you both," said the crow, "I shall show you the way."

Upon hearing the good news, Master Bruin, Sir Wolf and Bunny set about preparing for a bang-up feast. Bunny was appointed cook, for, having a short tail, it was less likely he would get scorched. Master Bruin, being the strongest amongst them, brought wood and game to the fireplace. The table was laid by Uncle Wolf who also acted as turnspit.

When dinner was ready, Sir Crow went to fetch the guests.

He flitted from tree to tree, but did not dare to alight on the ground and, perching on one of the trees, he called to the fox.

"Wait a minute, wait a bit! We shall soon be ready to start," said Reynard. "His Majesty is just twirling his moustache!"

It was not long before King Cat appeared in person. He stepped along with stately dignity, yet never lost sight of Sir Crow, of whom he was rather afraid. The crow, too, was scared and only ventured to look at him with one eye, as he led them, hopping from tree to tree, to the place appointed for the dinner.

Master Bruin, Uncle Wolf and Bunny were full of excitement and expectation. They kept asking themselves what sort of creature King Cat might turn out to be. They kept glancing down the road along which the guests were expected to arrive.

"There he comes, there he comes!" cried Bunny. "Ah, dear me, where shall I run to?" and, scared out of his wits, ran straight into the fire. Master Bruin, too, was seized with terror and rushed away, knocking his head against a tree so vigorously that the trunk split in two. Uncle Wolf bolted with the spit and the joint that was roasting on it. And Sir Crow, someone should live to tell the tale, followed their example.

The hungry guests found neither dinner nor hosts. Luckily, Bunny had in the meantime been so well roasted in the fire that they could pull him out and enjoy a hearty meal. And if they have not died, they are living happily to this day.

The Cat and the Mouse
[ENGLAND]

The cat and the mouse
Play'd in the malt-house:

The cat bit the mouse's tail off. "Pray, puss, give me my tail."

"No," says the cat, "I'll not give you your tail, till you go to the cow, and fetch me some milk."

First she leapt, and then she ran,
Till she came to the cow, and thus began:

"Pray, Cow, give me milk, that I may give cat milk, that cat may give me my own tail again."

"No," said the cow, "I will give you no milk, till you go to the farmer, and get me some hay."

First she leapt, and then she ran,
Till she came to the farmer, and thus began:

"Pray, farmer, give me hay, that I may give cow hay, that cow may give me milk, that I may give cat milk, that cat may give me my own tail again."

"No," says the farmer, "I'll give you no hay, till you go to the butcher and fetch me some meat."

First she leapt, and then she ran,
Till she came to the butcher, and thus began:

"Pray, Butcher, give me meat, that I may give farmer meat, that farmer may give me hay, that I may give cow hay, that cow may give me milk, that I may give cat milk, that cat may give me my own tail again."

"No," says the butcher, "I'll give you no meat, till you go to the baker and fetch me some bread."

First she leapt, and then she ran,
Till she came to the baker, and thus began:

"Pray, Baker, give me bread, that I may give butcher bread, that butcher may give me meat, that I may give farmer meat, that farmer may give me hay, that I may give cow hay, that cow may give me milk, that I may give cat milk, that cat may give me my own tail again."

"Yes," said the baker, "I'll give you some bread,
But if you eat my meal, I'll cut off your head."

Then the baker gave mouse bread, and mouse gave butcher bread, and butcher gave mouse meat, and mouse gave farmer meat, and farmer gave mouse hay, and mouse gave cow hay, and cow gave mouse milk, and mouse gave cat milk, and cat gave mouse her own tail again.

The Lazy Cat
[*HUNGARY*]

A lad once married a rich and lazy maid and solemnly promised he would never beat her.

The young woman did nary a stroke nor a stitch of work and day in day out cared for nought but tittle-tattle with neighbors near and far, or other idle pastimes. And still her man kept his word and never raised his hand against her. Yet one morning, before setting out to do his day's work, he turned to their cat and said: "Now, pussy, I command thee and bestir thyself and get to work while I am away; thou shalt tidy me up the house, thou shalt cook me the dinner and thou shalt spin me a reel of yarn as well. If the work be not done by the time I get home, I'll give thee such a whipping as thou'lt not forget in thy lifetime."

Dozing by the fireplace, the cat heard him out placidly, but the young woman, thinking her husband had taken leave of his senses, upbraided him thus:

"Why, my lord, do you bid this poor creature perform duties she knows nothing about?"

"I care not, woman, whether she knows or she doesn't," said the man and went on. "I have no one else to give orders to; but if she does not do as I have ordered, I shall beat her within an inch of her life!"

With this he went away and his wife began to urge the cat on, saying, "Work, pussy, work, for if thou dost not, my master will beat thee!"

But the cat did not work. So the woman went her way and after gossiping with the neighbors, returned to find the cat still dozing and the fire burned down.

"Mend that fire," she said to the cat, "and work, pussy, for thou wilt get thrashed!"

But the cat did not stir.

Home came the master and saw at a glance that nothing was done and everything ajumble. He picked up the cat, tied her to his wife's back and thrashed her till his wife implored him:

"Oh, oh! Stop beating that cat! It isn't her fault, she doesn't know how to do housework!"

"Will you promise then to do all the work in her stead?" asked her husband.

"I'll do even more than you have ordered if you will but stop beating that poor creature!" she replied.

And so the young woman ran home to her mother and complained about what had happened.

"I solemnly promise," she said, "to carry out all the duties thrust upon the cat, but let him cease whipping her!"

Her father, now, put in:

"He has given his promise, so you had better keep yours, or the cat will get another whipping tomorrow."

And thus he sent her home to her husband.

Next morning the master again ordered the cat to do this and that, and again the cat heard him out and did nothing. And so it came about that again he flogged her on his wife's back and again the young woman rushed home with her grievance. But this time her father sent her packing without further ado.

Came the third morning and with it the master's third order to the cat who, by that time, was so terrified that she could not even hear him out, let alone do any work. But now behold the young woman taking the place of the cat's and doing all the work herself, forgetting none of her promises: she lighted the fire, she fetched the water, she prepared the food, she swept the house, and she did all the work which had to be done—for, oh, how she pitied the poor dear cat who in her agony had kept digging her claws into her mistress' back, as her master thrashed her, whilst every stroke of the forked whip on the cat's back had also lashed the back of the woman.

When her husband came home and found everything tidy, he kept on saying to the cat:

"Have no fear, pussy, I'll not harm thee now!"

And his wife laid the table with pleasure, prepared a good repast and lovingly placed it before her husband. And, oh, what a meal it was and how they enjoyed it!

And thus it went on from that day forward; never again was the cat beaten, and the young woman became a housewife such as no one could match.

Three Wishes
[*UNITED STATES*]

There was once an old woman who lived alone with her cat. One night late, as she sat dozing in front of her fireplace, an elf suddenly appeared in front of her and startled her into wakefulness.

"Who are you? What do you want?" she asked.

The elf explained that he was there to grant her three wishes.

She was skeptical, but he persuaded her to tell him what she wished for.

She said, "First, I wish I were extremely rich. Second, I wish I were young and beautiful again. And third, I wish that my cat, lying beside me here on the couch, would become the handsomest young man in the world."

The elf assured her that her wishes would be granted, and then he disappeared. The old woman slipped back into her dozing.

Later she awakened and sensed that something was different. She looked around her, and, lo and behold! her house was elegantly furnished, everything was beautiful, expensive, and in its proper place! She was rich!

She rushed to the mirror and, lo! she was once again young and beautiful.

Then she remembered her third wish. She returned to the den, and sure enough, sitting there on the couch was the handsomest young man she had ever seen in her life. She sat down beside him, and as he put his arm around her, he said, "Now aren't you sorry you had me fixed?"

The Linguistic Cat
[ENGLAND]

Two mice were cowering in the mousehole while the cat approached.

"Miaow ... Miaow ... Miaaoow...." they heard.

Then "Woof ... Woof ... Woof...." the sound of a furious dog, a spitting retreat, and thankful silence.

Cautiously the two mice crept out of shelter—and the cat pounced on them, remarking as he ate them up:

"I always knew it would be useful to have a second language."

The Cat on the Dovrefell
[NORWAY]

Once upon a time there was a man up in Finnmark who had caught a great white bear, which he was going to take to the king of Denmark. Now, it so fell out, that he came to the Dovrefell just about Christmas Eve, and there he turned into a cottage where a man lived, whose name was Halvor, and asked the man if he could get houseroom there, for his bear and himself.

"Heaven never help me, if what I say isn't true!" said the man. "But we can't give any one houseroom just now, for every Christmas Eve such a pack of trolls come down upon us that we are forced to flit, and haven't so much as a house over our own heads, to say nothing of lending one to anyone else."

"Oh?" said the man, "if that's all, you can very well lend me your house; my bear can lie under the stove yonder, and I can sleep in the side room."

Well, he begged so hard that at last he got leave to stay there. So the people of the house flitted out, and before they went, everything was got ready for the trolls; the tables were laid, and there was rice porridge, and fish boiled in lye, and sausages, and all else that was good, just as for any other great feast.

So, when everything was ready, down came the trolls. Some were great, and some were small; some had long tails, and some had no tails at all; some, too, had long, long noses; and they ate and drank, and tasted everything. Just then one of the little trolls caught sight of the white bear, who lay under the stove; so he took a piece of sausage and stuck it on a fork, and went and poked it up against the bear's nose, screaming out:

"Pussy, will you have some sausage?"

Then the white bear rose up and growled, and hunted the whole pack of them out of doors, both great and small.

Next year Halvor was out in the wood, on the afternoon of Christmas Eve, cutting wood before the holidays, for he thought the trolls would come again; and just as he was hard at work, he heard a voice in the wood calling out:

"Halvor! Halvor!"

"Well," said Halvor, "here I am."

"Have you got your big cat with you still?"

"Yes, that I have," said Halvor. "She's lying at home under the stove, and what's more, she has now got seven kittens, far bigger and fiercer that she is herself."

"Oh, then, we'll never come to see you again," bawled out the troll away in the wood, and he kept his word; for since that time the trolls have never eaten their Christmas brose with Halvor on the Dovrefell.

A Few Wild Cousins

OUR FAMILIAR HOUSECAT was domesticated thousands of years ago (the earliest reference to domestic cats dates from around 1500 BCE, though of course the actual process may have taken place earlier). However, many of the world's cats remain wild—not only lions, tigers, leopards, and bobcats but even a European wildcat which looks very much like domesticated varieties. How the many types of cats, wild or domestic, should be scientifically classified and how they may be historically related to each other are matters that remain disputed.

What is certain, however, is that wild cats have had a powerful impact upon the human imagination—as fascinating creatures, as important symbols, as figures in literature and in folklore. Certainly there are many folktales about lions and tigers and leopards, and it seems only right to include in this book some stories about these untamed "cousins" of *Felis domesticus.*

Although such stories may present the wild cats in various guises, one theme is very prominent: the "taming" of these untamed beasts, by tricking them, caging them, or even by riding them. Of course humans fear the big cats, for wild felines can pose a threat—real or fancied—to human life and limb. The stories may function to provide an imaginary subduing of a dangerous, wild adversary and thus a symbolic, psychological victory over powerful natural forces by making the tiger or the lion seem, in the fictional world of the narrative, as easily handled as our own peaceful tabbies. In the process, however, humans do not always come out in a favorable light.

The Lion, the Jackal, and the Man
[SOUTH AFRICA]

*I*t so happened one day that Lion and Jackal came together to converse on affairs of land and state. Jackal, let me say, was the most important adviser to the king of the forest, and after they had spoken about these matters for quite a while, the conversation took a more personal turn.

Lion began to boast and talk big about his strength. Jackal had, perhaps, given him cause for it, because by nature he was a flatterer. But now that Lion began to assume so many airs, said he, "See here, Lion, I will show you an animal, called man, that is still more powerful than you are."

They walked along, Jackal leading the way, and met first a little boy.
"Is this the strong man?" asked Lion.
"No," answered Jackal, "he must still become a man, oh King."
After a while they found an old man walking with bowed head and supporting his bent figure with a stick.
"Is this the wonderful strong man?" asked Lion.
"Not yet, oh King," was Jackal's answer, "he has been a man."
Continuing their walk a short distance farther, they came across a

young hunter, in the prime of youth, and accompanied by some of his dogs.

"There you have him now, oh King," said Jackal. "Pit your strength against his, and if you win, then truly you are the strength of the earth."

Then Jackal made tracks to one side toward a little rocky kopje from which he would be able to see the meeting.

Growling, growling, Lion strode forward to meet the man, but when he came close the dogs beset him. He, however, paid but little attention to the dogs, pushed and separated them on all sides with a few sweeps of his front paws. They howled aloud, beating a hasty retreat toward the man.

Thereupon the man fired a charge of shot, hitting him behind the shoulder; but even to this Lion paid but little attention. Thereupon the hunter pulled out his steel knife, and gave him a few good jabs. Lion retreated, followed by the flying bullets of the hunter.

"Well, are you strongest now?" was Jackal's first question when Lion arrived at his side.

"No, Jackal," answered Lion, "let that fellow there keep the name and welcome. Such as he I have never seen before. In the first place he had about ten of his bodyguard storm me. I really did not bother myself much about them, but when I attempted to turn him to chaff, he spat and blew fire at me, mostly into my face, that burned just a little but not very badly. And when I again endeavored to pull him to the ground he jerked out from his body one of his ribs with which he gave me some very ugly wounds, so bad that I had to make chips fly, and as a parting he sent some warm bullets after me. No, Jackal, give him the name."

The Close Alliance: A Tale of Woe
[INDIA]

One day a farmer went with his bullocks to plough his field. He had just turned the first furrow, when a tiger walked up to him and said, "Peace be with you, friend! How are you this morning?"

"The same to you, my lord, and I am pretty well, thank you!" returned the farmer, quaking with fear, but thinking it wisest to be polite.

"I am glad to hear it," replied the tiger cheerfully, "because Providence has sent me to eat your two bullocks. You are a Godfearing man, I know, so make haste and unyoke them."

"My friend, are you sure you are not making a mistake?" asked the farmer, whose courage had returned now that he knew it was merely a question of gobbling up bullocks. "Because Providence sent me to plough this field, and, in order to plough, one must have oxen. Had you not better go and make further inquiries?"

"There is no occasion for delay, and I should be sorry to keep you waiting," returned the tiger. "If you'll unyoke the bullocks I'll be ready in a moment."

With that the savage creature fell to sharpening his teeth and claws in a very significant manner.

But the farmer begged and prayed that his oxen might not be eaten, and promised that if the tiger would spare them, he would give in exchange a fine fat young milch cow, which his wife had tied up in the yard at home.

To this the tiger agreed, and, taking the oxen with him, the farmer went sadly homewards. Seeing him return so early from the fields, his wife, who was a stirring, busy woman, called out, "What! lazybones!—back already, and *my* work just beginning!" Then the farmer explained how he had met the tiger and how to save the bullocks he had promised the milch cow in exchange. At this the wife began to cry, saying, "A likely story, indeed!—saving your stupid old bullocks at the expense of my beautiful cow! Where will the children get milk? And how can I cook my pottage and collops without butter?"

"All very fine, wife," retorted the farmer, "but how can we make bread without corn? And how can you have corn without bullocks to plough the fields? Pottage and collops are very nice, but it is better to do without milk and butter than without bread, so make haste and untie the cow."

"You great gaby!" wept the wife, "if you had an ounce of sense in your brain you'd think of some plan to get out of the scrape!"

"Think yourself!" cried the husband, in a rage.

"Very well!" returned the wife. "But if I do the thinking you must obey orders; I can't do both. Go back to the tiger, and tell him the cow wouldn't come along with you, but that your wife is bringing it."

The farmer, who was a great coward, didn't half like the idea of going back empty-handed to the tiger, but, as he could think of no other plan, he did as he was bid, and found the beast still sharpening his teeth and claws for very hunger. When he heard he had to wait still longer for his dinner, he began to prowl about, and lash his tail, and curl his whiskers, in a most terrible manner, causing the poor farmer's knees to knock together in terror.

Now, when the farmer had left the house, his wife went to the stable and saddled the pony; then she put on her husband's best clothes, tied the turban very high, so as to make her look as tall as possible, bestrode the pony, and set off to the field where the tiger was.

She rode along, swaggering and blustering, till she came to where the lane turned into the field, and then she called out, as bold as brass, "Now, please the powers! I may find a tiger in this place; for I haven't tasted tiger's meat since yesterday, when, as luck would have it, I ate three for breakfast."

Hearing these words, and seeing the speaker ride boldly at him, the tiger became so alarmed that he turned tail and bolted into the forest, going away at such a headlong pace that he nearly overturned his own jackal; for tigers always have a jackal of their own, who, as it were, waits at table and clears away the bones.

"My lord! my lord!" cried the jackal, "whither away so fast?"

"Run! run!" panted the tiger. "There's the very devil of a horseman in yonder fields, who thinks nothing of eating three tigers for breakfast!"

At this the jackal sniggered in his sleeve. "My dear lord," said he, "the sun has dazzled your eyes! That was no horseman, but only the farmer's wife dressed up as a man!"

"Are you quite sure?" asked the tiger, pausing.

"Quite sure, my lord," repeated the jackal. "And if your lordship's eyes had not been dazzled by—ahem!—the sun, your lordship would have seen her pigtail hanging down behind."

"But you may be mistaken!" persisted the cowardly tiger. "It was the very devil of a horseman to look at."

"Who's afraid?" replied the brave jackal. "Come! Don't give up your dinner because of a woman!"

"But you may be bribed to betray me!" argued the tiger, who, like all cowards, was suspicious.

"Let us go together, then!" returned the gallant jackal.

"Nay! But you may take me there and then run away!" insisted the tiger cunningly.

"In that case, let us tie our tails together, and then I can't."

The jackal, you see, was determined not to be done out of his bones.

To this the tiger agreed, and having tied their tails together in a reef knot, the pair set off arm-in-arm.

Now the farmer and his wife had remained in the field, laughing over the trick she had played on the tiger, when, lo and behold! what should they see but the gallant pair coming back ever so bravely, with their tails tied together.

"Run!" cried the farmer; "we are lost! we are lost!"

"Nothing of the kind, you grat gaby!" answered his wife coolly, "if you will only stop that noise and be quiet. I can't hear myself speak!"

Then she waited till the pair were within hail, when she called out politely, "How very kind of you, dear Mr. Jackal, to bring me such a nice fat tiger! I shan't be a moment finishing my share of him, and then you can have the bones."

At these words the tiger became wild with fright, and, quite forgetting the jackal, and that reef knot in their tails, he bolted away full tilt, dragging the jackal behind him. Bumpety, bump, bump, over the stones!—crash, scratch, patch, through the briars!

In vain the poor jackal howled and shrieked to the tiger to stop; the noise behind him only frightened the coward more; and away he went, helter-skelter, hurry-scurry, over hill and dale, till he was nearly dead with fatigue, and the jackal was *quite* dead from bumps and bruises.

The Brahman, the Tiger, and the Six Judges

[INDIA]

Once upon a time a brahman, who was walking along the road, came upon an iron cage, in which a great tiger had been shut up by the villagers who caught him.

As the brahman passed by, the tiger called out and said to him, "Brother Brahman, brother Brahman, have pity on me, and let me out of this cage for one minute only, to drink a little water, for I am dying of thirst."

The brahman answered, "No, I will not; for if I let you out of the cage you will eat me."

"Oh, father of mercy," answered the tiger, "in truth that I will not. I will never be so ungrateful; only let me out, that I may drink some water and return."

Then the brahman took pity on him, and opened the cage door; but no sooner had he done so than the tiger, jumping out, said, "Now, I will eat you first, and drink the water afterwards."

But the brahman said, "Only do not kill me hastily. Let us first ask the opinion of six, and if all of them say it is just and fair that you should put me to death, then I am willing to die."

"Very well," answered the tiger, "it shall be as you say. We will first ask the opinion of six."

So the brahman and the tiger walked on till they came to a banyan tree; and the brahman said to it, "Banyan tree, Banyan tree, hear and give judgment."

"On what must I give judgment?" asked the banyan tree.

"This tiger," said the brahman, "begged me to let him out of his cage to drink a little water, and he promised not to hurt me if I did so; but now that I have let him out he wishes to eat me. Is it just that he should do so, or no?"

The banyan tree answered, "Men often come to take refuge in the cool shade under my boughs from the scorching rays of the sun; but when they have rested, they cut and break my pretty branches, and wantonly scatter the leaves that sheltered them. Let the tiger eat the man, for men are an ungrateful race."

At these words the tiger would have instantly killed the brahman; but the brahman said, "Tiger, Tiger, you must not kill me yet, for you promised that we should first hear the judgment of six."

"Very well," said the tiger, and they went on their way. After a little while they met a camel.

"Sir Camel, Sir Camel," cried the brahman, "hear and give judgment."

"On what shall I give judgment?" asked the camel.

And the brahman related how the tiger had begged him to open the cage door, and promised not to eat him if he did so, and how he had afterwards determined to break his word and asked if that were just or not.

The camel replied, "When I was young and strong and could do much work, my master took care of me and gave me good food; but now that I am old, and have lost all my strength in his service, he overloads me, and starves me, and beats me without mercy. Let the tiger eat the man, for men are an unjust and cruel race."

The tiger would then have killed the brahman, but the latter said, "Stop, Tiger, for we must first hear the judgment of six."

So they both went again on their way. At a little distance they found a bullock lying by the roadside.

The brahman said to him, "Brother Bullock, brother Bullock, hear and give judgment."

"On what must I give judgment?" asked the bullock.

The brahman answered, "I found this tiger in a cage, and he prayed me to open the door and let him out to drink a little water, and promised not to kill me if I did so; but when I had let him out he resolved to put me to death. Is it fair he should do so or not?"

The bullock said, "When I was able to work, my master fed me well and tended me carefully, but now I am old he has forgotten all I did for him, and left me by the roadside to die. Let the tiger eat the man, for men have no pity."

Three out of the six had given judgment against the brahman, but still he did not lose all hope, and determined to ask the other three.

They next met an eagle flying through the air, to whom the brahman cried, "Oh Eagle, great Eagle, hear and give judgment."

"On what must I give judgment?" asked the eagle.

The brahman stated the case, but the eagle answered, "Whenever men see me they try to shoot me; they climb the rocks and steal away my little ones. Let the tiger eat the man, for men are persecutors of the earth."

Then the tiger began to roar, and said, "The judgment of all is against you, Oh Brahman."

But the brahman answered, "Stay a little longer, for two others must first be asked."

After this they saw an alligator, and the brahman related the matter to him, hoping for a more favorable verdict.

But the alligator said, "Whenever I put my nose out of the water, men torment me, and try to kill me. Let the tiger eat the man, for as long as men live we shall have no rest."

The brahman gave himself up as lost; but once more he prayed the tiger to have patience, and to let him ask the opinion of the sixth judge.

Now the sixth was a jackal. The brahman again told his story and said to him, "Uncle Jackal, uncle Jackal, say, what is your judgment?"

The jackal answered, "It is impossible for me to decide who is in the right and who in the wrong unless I see the exact position in which you were when the dispute began. Show me the place."

So the brahman and the tiger returned to the place where they first met, and the jackal went with them. When they got there, the jackal said, "Now, Brahman, show me exactly where you stood."

"Here," said the brahman, standing by the iron tiger-cage.

"Exactly there, was it?" asked the jackal.

"Exactly here," replied the brahman.

"Where was the tiger, then?" asked the jackal.

"In the cage," answered the tiger.

"How do you mean?" asked the jackal. "How were you within the cage, which way were you looking?"

"Why, I stood so," said the tiger, jumping into the cage, "and my head was on this side."

"Very good," said the jackal, "but I cannot judge without understanding the whole matter exactly. Was the cage door open or shut?"

"Shut, and bolted," said the brahman.

"Then shut and bolt it," said the jackal.

When the brahman had done this, the jackal said, "Oh, you wicked and ungrateful Tiger! When the good brahman opened your cage door, is to eat him the only return you would make? Stay there, then, for the rest of your days, for no one will ever let you out again. Proceed on your journey, friend Brahman. Your road lies that way, and mine this."

So saying, the jackal ran off in one direction, and the brahman went rejoicing on his way in the other.

Mrs. Cuttle and the Catamount
[UNITED STATES]

As narrated by Colonel David Crockett in **The Crockett Almanac** *of 1841.*

One day I fell in with Jo Cuttle. Jo war an honest ruff and tumble sort of a chap, and after we had jogged on a little way, sez he, "Kornel, thar war a pesky queer scrape once happened to me in these diggins. It war arter this sort: It war late one arternoon when my wife war cuming home from a tea-squall. She war passing rite thro' the forrest, and had forgot to bring her rifle with her. But she never were afeard of any thing less than a bull mammoth, and so she jogged along as merry and contented as a she bear. She cum to a deep hollow whar war a large pond of water, and she saw a big log lying near, and she rolled it in. As soon as the log war afloat, she got on one eend of it with her face towards the opposite shore, and begun to paddle across. When she got about haff way over, she happened to hear a low growl, and when she looked behind she saw that a great catamount sot on the other eend of the log. He had took passage with her when she first started, but she did not see him then.

"As my wife war sitting straddle, it took sum time for her to turn round, and face the catamount. He showed his teeth and grouled because she had left off paddling: so she concluded that he meant to behave civil, if she wood only carry him safe across; but she had an idee that arter they war fairly landed, he would try to make a breakfast of her. So she would not paddle another stroke. He kept grouling, as much as to say, 'Row away you infarnal jade!' That made her mad, for she cood understand his language jist as well as if she had been born to it; so she dashed water on him with her paddle. This made him wink a little, and he showed his teeth. When she seed he war going to spring rite at her, she just canted the log and he tumbled into the drink, but he put his paws up to get hold of the log agin, and kept trying to gain a foothold on it, which kept it turning round and round like a grindstone, till my wife's legs war chafed most ridiculous. At last she found she must get upon her feet, and then she war forced to keep hopping up and down all the time—she danced while the catamount fiddled upon the log. She then stomped on his paws, but he minded no more about that than a flea bite. So she watched a chance and gave a jump rite on the feller's back, and caught hold of both of his ears. When ever he tried to bite her, she wood bowse his head under and haff drown him. Then she set out to swim for the shore, and she kept upon his back, and guided him by pulling his right or left ear, jist as she wanted he shood go. Well, he got safe ashore with her, and she didn't dare let go of his ears, or to get off for fear he wood be into her like a buckshot.

"Now I happened to be out hunting, with one Kit Weatherblow, at this time, and Kit cum running to me, and told me he saw the strangest cretur going through the woods that he ever seed in his life before. He said it war a wild varmint in petticoats. I told Kit to go with me to hunt it up, for I had seen every cretur in the forrest, and this must be a stranger. We soon cum in sight of it, but I new my wife's petticoat as soon as I got a glimpse at it, and then I seed her head a little while arterward. So sez I to Kit, 'Sing dumb and let me get a blizzard at the obstropolous varmint, for he's running off with my wife.' I lifted my rifle and put a hole rite through his gizzard: but I shot away one of my wife's cap-strings at the same time, which war made of buffalo sinew. The varmint tumbled amongst the leaves pretty quick, and my wife picked herself off the ground in less than no time. When I seed she want hurt, I felt a little mad and told her never agin to clasp around the neck of any living thing but her own lawful husband."

Wildcat Gets a New Face
[NATIVE AMERICAN (Ute)]

Long ago Wildcat had a long nose and tail. One day he was sleeping on a rock when Coyote came along. He pushed Wildcat's nose and tail in, and then went home. At noon Wildcat woke up and noticed his short nose and tail.

"What's the matter with me?" he asked. Then he guessed the cause. "Oh! Coyote did that," he said, and he hunted for him.

Now, Coyote was sleepy and had lain down. Wildcat came and sat beside him. He pulled out Coyote's nose and tail and made them long. They were short before. Then he ran off. After a while Coyote woke up and saw *his* long nose and tail.

Tiger and Bra Nansi
[WEST INDIES (San Andreas)]

Bra Nansi or Anansi is the spider, the trickster figure in many African and Afro-Caribbean folktales.

Here is the tale of Bra Nansi's old riding horse.

Tiger and Anansi were fond of the same girls, but Tiger was not as cunning as Anansi. Tiger was very handsome and he used to visit the girls every week. Nansi noticed how the two girls were becoming sweet on Tiger.

One day Anansi went to the girls' house and said, "Girls, I'll show you that Tiger is only my father's old riding horse."

"How is that?" they said.

"Next time I come to call on you, you will see," he said.

The next Sunday Tiger visited the girls; they told him what Anansi had said. Tiger flew into a rage and went running in search of Anansi. Tiger arrived at Anansi's house and knocked on the door. He was plenty vexed.

Anansi called in a very weak voice, "Yeeeas, whooo there?"

Tiger demanded to be let in. Anansi, lying in bed, told him to enter. Anansi said he would like to offer Tiger tea, but he was feeling so poorly right now he couldn't rise.

Tiger asked why Anansi had told the girls that he was only Anansi's father's riding horse. Tiger told Anansi that he wanted him to come and tell the girls that what he had said was untrue.

Anansi said, "I never said it, and I would come, but I can't walk at all."

"I'll tell you what," said Tiger. "If I carry you on my back, will you come?"

"Well, if you insist, I will do it," said Anansi.

Anansi climbed on Tiger's back, but acted as if he was too weak and would fall off.

"You'll have to get my saddle," said Anansi.

"Okay, I'll do anything, just so you come," said Tiger.

Next, Anansi had Tiger get the bridle.

"What you going to do with that?" asked Tiger.

"That's so if I start to fall, I can catch up," replied Anansi.

Tiger started to go, but after a few steps Anansi fell off.

"I can't stay on your back without those little things called spurs," cried Anansi.

"Okay, okay, I don't care what you do. Let's get on with it," said Tiger.

As they were riding towards the girls' house, they went through a wood.

"Hold up here, one minute," said Anansi. "I need to cut a whip so I can let you know when to go slower."

Tiger agreed, and finally they got near to the girls' yard.

No sooner were they at the girls' yard than Anansi began whipping Tiger with his whip and juked him hard with his spurs. Tiger let out a yell and began to run as fast as he could. Anansi waved to the girls, then jumped off Tiger's back and climbed up onto the veranda.

"You see, Tiger is not only my father's old riding horse, but for me also."

And Tiger was so ashamed, he ran into the woods and didn't return.

Jack Mandora, me no choose none.

Afterword

SOME FURTHER INFORMATION

Several good books deal with cats in relation to society and culture, including folklore. Patricia Dale-Green, *Cult of the Cat* (Boston: Houghton Mifflin Co., 1963) considers many of the cat's social aspects over the long span of history and explores various facets of mythology, belief, and behavior. Mildred Kirk, *The Everlasting Cat* (Woodstock, New York: Overlook Press, 1985) also ably surveys the social history of felines and includes a short chapter on several of the more important folktales about cats. The noted English folklorist Katharine M. Briggs, in *Nine Lives: The Folklore of Cats* (New York: Pantheon Books, 1980), produced a notable study of the lore of cats, concentrating primarily upon narratives but also taking up questions of folk belief. Earlier the mythologist Angelo de Gubernatis, in *Zoological Mythology; or the Legends of Animals* (London: Trübner & Co., 1872; 2 vols.) had turned his attention to the folk narrative material concerning cats, but his remarks, though certainly of interest, are surprisingly brief, limited to only part of a chapter in volume 2. For particular folk beliefs (superstitions) about cats, the recent book edited by Iona Opie and Moira Tatem, *A Dictionary of Superstitions* (Oxford and New York: Oxford University Press, 1989), is a useful guide, giving references to the original sources of their own information. Collections of superstitions, such as volume 7 of *The Frank C. Brown Collection of North Carolina Folklore*, ed. Newman Ivey White et al (Durham: Duke University Press, 1952) and *Popular Beliefs and Superstitions: A Compendium of American Folklore from the Ohio Collection of Newbell Niles Puckett*, ed. Wayland D. Hand, Anna Casetta, and Sondra B. Thiederman (Boston: G. K. Hall & Co., 1981), include many items relating to cats.

A great deal has been written about folk narratives. Stith Thompson, *The Folktale* (New York: Holt, Rinehart & Winston, 1946), is the standard discussion of fictional tales (such as fairy tales and jocular tales), though its purview is limited mostly to tales in the Indo-European languages. More recently Max Lüthi has provided illuminating discussion of folk narrative in several books which have been translated into English from his native German. In *Once Upon a Time: On the Nature of Fairy Tales*

(Bloomington, Indiana, and London: Indiana University Press, 1970) he draws distinctions between different types of folktales and discusses the psychology—broadly speaking—of fairy tales in particular. His *The Fairytale as Art From and Portrait of Man* (Bloomington: Indiana University Press, 1984) deals with the aesthetics and the social position of fairy tales, and *The European Folktale: Form and Nature* (Philadelphia: Institute for Study of Human Issues, 1982) examines the fairy tale as a "particular kind of literary artifact." In such books as *Fairy Tales and The Art of Subversion: The Classical Genre for Children and the Process of Civilization* (New York: Wildman Press, 1983) and *Breaking the Magic Spell: Radical Theories of Folk and Fairy Tales* (Austin: University of Texas Press, 1979), Jack Zipes has written on the social history and "politics" of fairy tales, including the use of such tales by writers.

Perhaps the most widely read book on fairy tales in recent years is Bruno Bettelheim's *The Uses of Enchantment: The Meaning and Importance of Fairy Tales* (New York: Alfred A. Knopf, 1976), in which this psychologist argues that hearing fairy tales is highly beneficial for children because they receive supportive messages from the stories. However, to obtain an excellent presentation of the world in which fairy tales and other oral narratives live, i.e., of the social context of tale-telling, one should read Linda Dégh's *Folktales and Society: Story-Telling in a Hungarian Peasant Community* (Bloomington: Indiana University Press, 1969), which deals with life in a culture where tale-telling is an important reality, with the occasions when stories are told and the personalities of several narrators. In *Folklore by the Fireside: Text and Context of the Tuscan Veglia* (Austin: University of Texas Press, 1980) Alessandro Falassi provides an excellent description and analysis of the *veglia* in Italy, an evening gathering of family and friends at which various kinds of folklore, including stories, were performed and exchanged. W.R. Geddes, *Nine Dayak Nights* (Oxford: Oxford University Press, 1961), also provides a vivid picture of how tales are told, dealing with the narration not of a fairy tale but of a tribal legend by a shaman of the headhunting Land Dayaks in Borneo. The Folktales of the World series, published in the United States by the University of Chicago Press, is an excellent source of folktale texts from oral tradition; different volumes cover different countries.

Legends of the "contemporary" or "urban" variety have been the subject of a number of books by Jan Harold Brunvand, including *The Vanishing Hitchhiker: American Urban Legends and Their Meanings* (New York: W. W. Norton & Co., 1981) and *The Choking Doberman and Other "New" Urban Legends* (New York: W. W. Norton & Co., 1984), although for the views of contemporary American folklorists on legends in general, one needs to look at the various essays in *American Folk Legend: A Symposium*, ed. Wayland D. Hand (Berkeley and Los Angeles: University of California Press, 1971). Humorous stories—though most particularly jokes—have also been given attention by folklorists and others. Sigmund Freud himself produced the classic *Jokes and Their Relation to the Unconscious*, trans. James Strachey (New York: W. W. Norton & Co., 1960) and both Alan Dundes, *Cracking Jokes: Studies of Sick Humor Cycles and Stereotypes* (Berkeley: Ten Speed Press, 1987), and Elliott Oring, *Jokes and Their Relations* (Lexington: University of Kentucky Press, 1992), contain many insightful observations on these forms of folklore.

Much information on publications about folk stories can be found in the annually published *MLA International Bibliography of Books and Articles on the Modern Languages and Literatures* (which includes a folklore section), and the *International Folklore Bibliography* (published in Germany).

Because different variations of the same folktales are told in many different cultures and places, folklorists have been able to extensively catalogue many of the world's oral narratives via systems which give a particular tale a number and a generic title. Various indexes published in accord with these systems are useful to those who wish to find various versions of a particular story (each such story, such as "Puss in Boots," which may be found told all over the world in different variations, is called a tale type.) The basic numbering system is that found in Antti Aarne and Stith Thompson, *The Types of the Folktale: A Classification and Bibliography* (Helsinki: Suomalainan Tiedeakatemia, Academia Scientiarum Fennica, 1961; vol. 184 in the FF Communications series), which gives references to texts of tales in many languages. Easier to use for those seeking texts only in English, however, is D.L. Ashliman, *A Guide to Folktales in the English Language* (Westport, Connecticut, and London: Greenwood Press, 1987). Particular elements of folk stories (such as "Cat as beast of ill omen"), referred to as motifs, have been classified by Stith Thompson in his multi-volume *Motif-Index of Folk-Literature* (Bloomington: Indiana University Press, 1955-58). Motifs are used as an organizing principle in the very useful guide to folklore in books meant primarily for children, *The Storyteller's Sourcebook: A Subject, Title, and Motif Index to Folklore Collections for Children*, ed. Margaret Read MacDonald (Detroit: Gale Research Co., 1982).

For the convenience of those who may wish to know more about the stories found in this book, information is provided just below; it includes references to tale types (the abbreviation AT, for Aarne and Thompson, is used before the relevant number), and to some motifs (the word *Motif* before a capital letter and a combination of numbers).

The Cat and the Mouse in Partnership, from Andrew Lang, *The Yellow Fairy Book* (London: Longmans, 1894).

AT 15, *The Theft of Butter (Honey) by Playing Godfather*. The identity of the trickster in this story varies widely; for example, Richard M. Dorson, *American Negro Folktales* (Greenwich, Connecticut: Fawcett, 1967), pp. 68-79, gives several versions in which the culprit is Brother Rabbit, the character popular in many African-American stories.

Four of Aesop's Fables

"A Cat and Venus," from Sir Nicholas L'Estrange, *Fables of Aesop and Other Eminent Mythologists* (London: R. Sare, 1694).

Motif J1908.2, *Cat transformed to maiden runs after mouse*.

"The Eagle, the Cat, and the Sow," from Thomas Bewick, *The Fables of Aesop and Others* (Newcastle: T. Bewick & Son, 1818).

Motif K2131.1, *Cat brings suspicion between eagle and sow*.

"The Cat and the Fox," from Thomas Bewick, *The Fables of Aesop and Others* (Newcastle: T. Bewick & Son, 1818).

AT 105, *The Cat's Only Trick*.

"Belling the Cat," from Joseph Jacobs, *The Fables of Aesop* (New York: Macmillan, 1894).

AT 110, *Belling the Cat*.

In ancient Greece various animal fables were commonly attributed to Aesop, probably a semi-legendary person. The first known collection of Aesopic stories was put together in the 4th century BCE, although a Latin collection assembled by Phaedrus in the 1st century was most influential with later writers. Many of the Aesopic stories, however, have continued to be a part of oral tradition in some from or other.

The King o' the Cats, from Joseph Jacobs, *More English Fairy Tales* (London: D. Nutt, 1894).

AT 113A, *King of the Cats Is Dead*. In his *The Crayon Miscellany* (New York: G.P. Putnam, 1868), pp. 271-72, Washington Irving writes of Sir Walter Scott's telling him this story when Irving visited Scott's home, Abbotsford. It gives the reader some sense of a real taletelling situation and how tales may be recounted in particular contexts under particular circumstances.

Why the Cat Falls on Her Feet, from Louise Jean Walker, *Legends of Green Hill Sky* (Grand Rapids, Michigan: Wm. B. Eerdmans, 1959).

The domestic cat was not known in North America until the arrival of Europeans, so there are few Native American tales about the creatures. Walker apparently heard this story in Michigan where her family became acquainted with local Native Americans.

Why the Leopard Can Only Catch Prey on Its Left Side, from W.H. Barker and Cecilia Sinclair, *West African Folk-Tales* (London: G.G. Harrap, 1917).

Motifs A2463.1, *Why leopard cannot capture animal who passes him on right side*, A2581, *Why tiger lacks some quality of cats; cat, his teacher, omitted to teach him all he knew*. This second motif is widespread in Asia and seems in this tale also applicable in the context of the African leopard. Maung Htin Aung, *Burmese Folk-Tales* (Calcutta: Oxford University Press, 1948), gives a version, pp. 18-21.

The Cat and the "Jam," from Manuel J. Andrade, *Folk-lore from the Dominican Republic* (New York: American Folklore Society, 1930; Memoirs of the American Folklore Society, vol 23). Translated from the Spanish by Juan Barroso VIII.

AT105*, *Cat's Curiosity and Single Trick*. Terrence Leslie Hansen, *The Types of the Folktale in Cuba, Puerto Rico, the Dominican Republic, and Spanish South America* (Berkeley and Los Angeles: University of California Press, 1957) denotes it Type **218A and provides several references.

The Cat, the Dog, and Death, from Harold Courlander, *The Piece of Fire and Other Haitian Tales* (New York: Harcourt, Brace & World, 1942).

Motifs A1335, *Origin of death*, A1335.1.1, *Origin of death: wrong messenger goes to God*. The Haitian story seems to have African roots, for similar accounts are found in African cultures. Alice Werner, *Myths and Legends of the Bantus* (London: G.G. Harrap, 1933), pp. 31-33, provides other accounts, and Richard C. Bundy, "Folk-Tales from Liberia," *Journal of American Folklore* 32 (1919): 408, gives a text in which Cat is responsible for death because he forgets powerful medicine he has been sent for to ward death off.

The Master Cat; or Puss in Boots, from Andrew Lang, *The Blue Fairy Book* (London: Longmans, 1889), adapted from Charles Perrault's famous collection of 1697, *Contes de ma mère l'oye*.

AT 545B, *Puss in Boots*. This story has been very widely known in part because of its inclusion in literary tale collections, including such early ones as Perrault's and Giambattista Basile's *Pentamerone*. It continues to be very popular. A recent retelling by Lincoln Kirstein (Boston: Little, Brown, 1992), for example, contains lovely illustrations by Alain Vaës.

The White Cat, from Andrew Lang, *The Blue Fairy Book* (London: Longmans, 1889), adapted from a collection made by Madame d'Aulnoy.

AT 402, *The Mouse (Cat, Frog, etc.) as Bride*. This story is popular in many languages, although transformation into a mouse or frog seems more common than into a cat. The author of the long, literary version used here, Marie Catherine, Comtesse d'Aulnoy (1649-1705), was one of several 17th century French writers who published fairytales for a reading public fond of short, elegant narratives; she also wrote memoirs and travel accounts.

The Cat Who Became a Queen, from J.H. Knowles, *Folk-Tales of Kashmir* (London: Paul, Trench, Trübner, 1893).

Motifs B601.12, *Marriage to cat*, D342, *Transformation: cat to person*. Collected in Kashmir from a narrator called Rázi.

The Colony of Cats, from Andrew Lang, *The Crimson Fairy Book* (London: Longmans, 1903).

AT 403, *The Black and the White Bride*, which is closely related to AT 480, *The Spinning-Woman by the Spring; The Kind and the Unkind Girls*. Lang does not provide his original source, but from the names used, the tale appears to be Italian. Although the residents of the place to which the girls go in these tales are usually not cats, there are several Italian variants in which they are. See Italo Calvino, *Italian Folktales*, trans. George Martin (New York: Harcourt, Brace, Jovanovich, 1980), pp. 446-48, and Elizabeth Mathias and Richard Raspa, *Italian Folktales in America: The Verbal Art of an Immigrant Woman* (Detroit: Wayne State University, 1985), pp. 95-102.

Whittington and his Cat, from Edwin Sidney Hartland, *English Fairy and Other Folk Tales* (London: Walter Scott, 1890).

AT 1651, *Whittington's Cat*. As was noted in the introduction, this widespread folktale has been attached, in England, to the historical figure of Sir Richard Whittington. In other versions the hero sometimes inherits his cat, as when this tale is joined in the telling with the closely-related AT 1650, *The Three Lucky Brothers*, a motif found also in *Puss in Boots*.

How Raja Rasâlu Played *Chaupur* with King Sarkap, from Flora Annie Steel, *Tales of the Punjab* (London: Macmillan, 1894).

AT 217, *The Cat and the Candle*. Steel's text, however, is apparently a prose rendering of an episode from the cycle of songs sung about the legendary hero Raja Rasâlu in the Punjab region of northern India. As seems clear from the story itself, *chaupur* is a board game; each player has eight pieces on a cross-shaped board and the moves are determined by throwing dice.

The Bremen Town-Musicians, from *Grimm's Household Tales*, ed. and trans. Margaret Hunt, 2 vols. (London: Bohn, 1884).

AT 130, *The Animals in Night Quarters*.

The Cat and the Two Sorceresses, from F.M. Luzel, *Contes populaires de Basse-Bretagne*, 3 vols. (Paris: Maisonneuve & Ch. Leclerc, 1887). Translated from the French by Frank de Caro.

AT 708, *The Wonder-Child*.

Catskin, from Ernest Rhys, *Fairy Gold: A Book of Old English Fairy Tales* (London: J.M. Dent, 1907).

As found in the oral traditions of the world, the story commonly called "Cinderella" is actually a complex of related stories generally classified as AT 510 (then broken down into 510A, *Cinderella*, and 510B, *The Dress of Gold, of Silver, and of Stars* [*Cap o' Rushes*]), and AT 511, *One Eye, Two Eyes, Three Eyes*. "Catskin" is a variant of 510B, a tale in which the protagonist receives dresses or costumes made of various unusual materials, not only catskin. However, cats seem to be related to the story in various other ways. In some versions (including that in Basile's seventeenth-century *Pentamerone*) the main character is named Hearth Cat or something similar (because of her lowly position in the household, she is covered by ashes and cinders, like a cat who sleeps by the hearth of the fire), and in Norwegian and Irish versions of the story she is helped by a cat. The song quoted in the story is a verse version of "Catskin" found in James Orchard Halliwell, *The Nursery Rhymes of England* (London: J.R. Smith, 1843), pp. 65-74, which Halliwell notes as having been recorded from the recitation or singing of an 81-year-old woman. Rhys' version seems to be a prose rendering of this poem.

The Witch Cat, from F.A. de Caro, "The Witch Cat," *Indiana Folklore* 1 (1968).

Motifs D702.1.1, *Cat's paw cut off; woman's hand missing*, G252, *Witch in form of cat has hand cut off*, H57, *Recognition by missing member*, G211. *Witch in animal form*. Legends of witches in cat form are widespread, in the United States as elsewhere. Christine Goldberg, "Traditional American Witch Legends: A Catalog," *Indiana Folklore* 7 (1974): 86-89, gives references to many examples. She sees the witch cat as one of several major types of American witch legends.

The Baldheaded Cat of Kowashi, from Yoshimatsu Suzuki, *Japanese Legends and Folk-Tales* (Tokyo: Sakuri Shoten, 1949).

As no bald head is mentioned in the text, the title seems unexplained!

The Cats of San Lorenzo, from Charles Godfrey Leland, *Legends of Florence* (London: D. Nutt, 1895).

See notes to "The Witch Cat," "The Witch Cat in the Mill," and "The Demon Cat" for information on the connection between cats and witches and the devil. The church of San Lorenzo was begun in 1420 and was the family church of the Medicis; its cloister was indeed the city's home for stray felines, who were fed with scraps collected daily throughout Florence. It is located not far from the *Duomo* (cathedral).

The Vampire Cat of Nabéshima, from A.B. Mitford, *Tales of Old Japan* (London: Macmillan, 1871).

Motif G351.2, *Cat as ogre; sucks blood*. Mitford may have drawn this text from popular literary sources, for he alludes to "Japanese storybooks" as a source. Contrary to the ending of the story as given here, Patricia Dale-Green, *The Cult of the Cat*, p. 108, notes a 1929 newspaper report of belief in appearances of this cat-vampire in Japan at that time. The creature in the story seems not be a vampire quite in the sense in which this term is generally used—that is, a member of the "living dead" who sucks humans' blood—rather, it refers to a sort of "spiritual" sucking away of the human life force. Mitford notes that the belief in the power of certain animals to assume human form to work evil or good is widespread in Japanese folklore. Hizen, actually, was one of several powerful "baronies" during the period of the Tokugawa shoguns (1603-1867), Nabéshima being the name of the noble family who were its lords. A.B. Mitford became Lord Redesdale in 1902 and was the grandfather of writers Nancy and Jessica Mitford.

King Arthur's Fight with the Great Cat, from Lady Wilde, *Ancient Legends, Mystic Charms, and Superstitions of Ireland*, 2 vols. (Boston: Ticknor, 1887).

Motifs, B871.1.6, *Giant cat*, B16.1.1, *Monster cat devastates country*; Motif 126.1, *Giant ogre in the shape of a cat* is of relevance. Lady Wilde gives her source as a 15th century prose romance, so the original oral nature of the story is somewhat conjectural.

The Demon Cat, from Lady Wilde, *Ancient Legends, Mystic Charms, and Superstitions of Ireland*, 2 vols. (Boston: Ticknor, 1887).

Motifs G303.3.3.1.2, *Devil in form of a cat*, B147.1.2.2, *Cat as beast of ill omen*. James Travis, "Three Irish Folktales," *Journal of American Folklore* 54 (1941): 202-203, gives a story told to his Irish-American father by *his* Irish-born mother in which a priest exorcises a devil in cat form, though there the cat is owned by Protestants who dote on it. Sean O'Sullivan, *Legends from Ireland* (Totowa, New Jersey: Rowman & Littlefield, 1978), pp. 23-25, also provides a legend text in which a priest exorcises a devil-cat from a Protestant-owned castle, occasioning the conversion of its owner to Catholicism.

The Story of the Faithful Cat, from A.B. Mitford, *Tales of Old Japan* (London: Macmillan, 1871).

Motif B524.1.3, *Cat kills attacking rat*.

Who Let the Cat Out of the Bag in Austin, Texas, from *The Texan Woman*, 1, no. 3 (1974).

This short story by Diane Rutt uses the well-known "contemporary" legend which folklorists have called "The Dead Cat in the Package." Brunvand provides texts and discusses the legend in *The Vanishing Hitchhiker*, pp. 103-112, *The Choking Doberman*, pp. 129, 216-19, *The Mexican Pet: More "New" Urban Legends and Some Old Favorites* (New York: W.W. Norton, 1981, 1984, and 1986, respectively), pp. 31-34. In 1988 Jack Smith published a newspaper column with a story in which the protagonist runs over the beloved cat of a friend whose lovely apartment he has borrowed while the friend is away; he has to race around to pet stores to find a matching replacement. See the indexes to Brunvand's books for other references to cats; he has also mentioned other cat legends in his syndicated columns (syndicated by United Feature Syndicate, although now discontinued) distributed for release on September 28, 1989, April 23, 1990, and February 10, 1992.

King Cat, from Gyula Ortutay, *Hungarian Folk Tales* (Budapest: Corvina, 1962).

AT 103, *The Wild Animals Hide from the Unfamiliar Animal*, and AT 103A*, *Cat Claims to be King and Receives Food from Other Animals*.

The Cat and the Mouse, from Joseph Jacobs, *English Fairy Tales* (London: D. Nutt, 1890).

AT 2032, *The Cock's Whiskers*. A version of this story appearing in a collection of Italian tales (translated into English) was read to a group of Zuñi Indians by the anthropologist Frank Hamilton Cushing; later Cushing collected a much-changed version from one of his listeners. The comparison of the two versions (reprinted in Alan Dundes, ed., *The Study of Folklore* [Englewood Cliffs, New Jersey: Prentice-Hall, 1965], pp. 269-76) is a fascinating introduction to what may happen to folk stories which pass orally from one culture to another.

The Lazy Cat, from Gyula Ortutay, *Hungarian Folk Tales* (Budapest: Corvina, 1962).

AT 1370, *The Lazy Wife*. The theme of a husband who obeys the letter of a promise to his wife's family by beating her indirectly is also well-known from the English and American ballad, "The Wife Wrapt in Wether's Skin."

Three Wishes, contributed by Joseph Goodwin.

The joke parodies such Motifs as F341, *Fairies give fulfillment of wishes* and D1761, *Magic results produced by wishing*. Heard by Mr. Goodwin in Indiana in the early 1980s, told to him by a cat owner.

The Linguistic Cat, from Pass the Port: *The Best After-Dinner Stories of the Famous* (Cirencester, England: Christian Brann, 1976).

Motifs K810, *Fatal deception into trickster's power*, K1800, *Deception by disguise or illusion*. Contributed by Professor Donald M. MacKay.

The Cat on the Dovrefell, from George W. Dasent, *Popular Tales from* *the Norse* (London: George Routledge & Sons, 1907).

AT 1161, *The Bear Trainer and His Bear*. The Dovrefell is properly the Dovre Fjeld, a little inhabited plateau in central Norway, noted in folklore as a residence of trolls (in Scandinavian lore, strange, sometimes dangerous, cave-dwelling beings). Finnmark is a county in the Norwegian far north.

The Lion, the Jackal, and the Man, from James A. Honeij, *South African Folk-Tales* (New York: Baker & Taylor, 1910).

AT 157, *Learning to Fear Man*.

The Close Alliance: A Tale of Woe, from Flora Annie Steel, *Tales of the Punjab* (London: Macmillan, 1894).

Motif K235.1.1, *Husband promises a cow to tiger; wife frightens the tiger away*, K1719, *Ogre (large animal) overawed*, J1706.1, *Tiger as stupid beast*, J2132.5.1, *Other animal's tail tied to tiger's (leopard's); killed when tiger flees*.

The Brahman, the Tiger, and the Six Judges, from Mary Frere, *Old Deccan Days* (London: John Murray, 1870).

AT 155, *The Ungrateful Serpent Returned to Captivity*.

Mrs. Cuttle and the Catamount, from *The Crockett Almanac 1841* (Nashville: Ben Harding, 1841).

The Crockett almanacs were popular publications which played a role in the shaping of American humor. They were one source of humorous sketches about comic-heroic frontiersmen (including a fictionalized Davy Crockett) and about (comically exaggerated) conceptions of life on the frontier, especially the Old Southwest. Though works of popular literature, they drew upon the oral lore of the region and upon such forms as the tall tale. The term *catamount* is used to refer to several types of wild cats.

Wildcat Gets a New Face, from J. Alden Mason, "Myths of the Uintah Utes," *Journal of American Folklore* 23 (1910).

Motifs A2213.4.1, *Coyote's muzzle pulled out long*, A2335.4.4, *Why coyote has long muzzle*. In the tales of many North American Indian groups coyote is the trickster figure. In *Humor and Laughter: An Anthropological Approach* (Ithaca and London: Cornell University Press, 1985), p. 214, Mahadev Apte notes that the "trickster is both buffoon and culture hero," for in the narratives he acts irresponsibly infantile, yet also has supernatural powers and acquires for humanity many of the basic aspects of life, such as fire and water (or, as here, the form of the wildcat). The trickster is thus an incongruous and puzzling figure in folklore.

Tiger and Bra Nansi, collected on San Andreas Island and adapted from a modified Jamaican Creole by Jay D. Edwards.

Motif J1706.1, *Tiger as stupid beast*. As Coyote is the trickster figure for many Native American groups, so Anansi, the spider, figures as the trickster in African and Afro-Caribbean tales, though Brother (or Brer) Rabbit generally assumes the same role in the African-American stories of the United States. "Jack Mandora, me no choose none" is the closing formula (like "They lived happily ever after") which means that the story is not meant to apply to or be about anyone listening to it.